A LEADER'S GUIDE
TO SOLVING CHALLENGES WITH

EMOTIONAL
INTELLIGENCE

Updated Version

A Leader's Guide to Solving Challenges with Emotional Intelligence
Updated Version
by David R. Caruso and Lisa T. Rees

First published by EI Skills Group in 2021
www.LTRleadership.com
www.eiskills.com
blueprint@eiskills.com

ISBN: 978-1-945028-20-5

Book design and production assistance by Adam Robinson
for GoodBookDevelopers.com

A LEADER'S GUIDE TO SOLVING CHALLENGES WITH EMOTIONAL INTELLIGENCE

Updated Version

David R. Caruso PhD

Lisa T. Rees PCC, MPA

EI Skills Group
2021

CONTENTS

PREFACE

WE BELIEVE NOW, MORE THAN EVER, THE SKILLS OF emotional intelligence are what we need to repair our world. Since first writing this book, we, like you perhaps, have experienced a range of intense emotions, including sadness and anger, and perhaps relief, excitement and hope, as we make sense of the world around us. We know effective leaders, leaders who can guide us through these difficult times, are those who possess strong emotional intelligence.

We have updated this book, and have published a hands-on skill-building guide, Developing Your Emotional Intelligence Skills, to assist leaders, educators, team members, committee chairs and future leaders in getting things done by creating climates of respect where everyone's voice can be heard. Additionally, we updated some of the original book material, expanded areas to add more context, and added a new blueprint to reflect our changing environment.

Bottom line, we need leaders with empathy and compassion who are inspiring and hopeful for a better tomorrow. Leaders who have moral courage, leaders who feel our joy and our pain and leaders who generate conditions which enable us to achieve our goals. We encourage you to build your emotional intelligence skills by reading this book, but more importantly, practicing it and sharing it with others. Thank you for all you do to make the world a better place.

David C. Caruso, New Haven, CT
Lisa T. Rees, Burlington, VT

INTRODUCTION

OVER THE YEARS WE HAVE OBSERVED AND COACHED many leaders who were intelligent and hard-working but struggled to lead individuals, teams or their organization. There are many ways to lead, and there are many skills and traits successful leaders possess. Foremost, we believe that great leaders have the ability to accurately read emotions, to harness the power of emotions, to understand the causes of emotions and to effectively manage emotions. In other words, they possess a high level of emotional intelligence.

Leaders are hired to lead change because change-averse organizations become obsolete and irrelevant. That is why organizations need leaders who embrace change, lead change and thrive on change. The Center for Creative Leadership (CCL) reported on an IBM study where 1,500 CEO's were interviewed on the future of leadership development[1]. Their number one concern and worry is that today's leaders are ill-equipped to lead in volatile, uncertain, complex and ambiguous conditions. Therefore, helping leaders develop skills they need to successfully navigate and thrive in complex work environments is more important now than ever. In fact, that same CCL white paper talks about the importance of other skills—skills beyond technical competencies. The World Economic Forum notes that emotional intelligence is one

---

1   IBM, Capitalizing on Complexity: Insights from the Global Chief Executive Officer Study, Retrieved from https://www-01.ibm.com/common/ssi/cgi-bin/ssialias?htmlfid=GBE03297USEN.

1

of the 10 required skills for the future workforce[2]. We, too, believe the emotional intelligence skills we teach in this book are some of the many skills required to be a great leader.

We assume you have superb technical know-how, a high level of intelligence and are fully engaged with the work. We assume you have process maps and dashboards for major initiatives. However, you may not have highly-developed skills to figure out how your people are embracing (or rejecting) work priorities and the impact emotions are having on reaching organizational goals. This is why we wrote this book.

This is not a leadership book per se, but rather a book about utilizing the skills of emotional intelligence as a leader, and as a follower. The highly emotionally-intelligent leader is in their position to make a positive difference in the world, not to wield power. There are many books on emotional intelligence and even more on leadership. They all have important things to offer. *This book is designed to provide you—in the most efficient way possible—with practical skills and tips to leverage emotions to help you become a more effective leader.*

This book is for those who believe being a great leader is about building trust and forging strong relationships that include emotional connections. Yet, emotions are multi-faceted and incredibly complex and emotional intelligence provides you with a skill set to harness their power. While emotions help us develop trust, emotions can also derail us from achieving success. Emotions can energize us but many leaders feel overwhelmed by emotions they and others are experiencing, unsure how to deal effectively with emotions—especially emotions they label as "negative". You will see us embrace all emotions rather than blindly encouraging the

---

2   https://www.weforum.org/agenda/2016/01/the-10-skills-you-need-to-thrive-in-the-fourth-industrial-revolution/.

development of "happy" leaders. The emphasis on positive emotions in the last several years may be a reaction to psychology's historical focus on illness but it may also have gone too far. There are times when anxiety is smart and effective, such as when you are readying yourself for a major presentation to the board. There are times when anger is justified, such as when a competitor disses your new product line[3]. By being smart about emotions, by knowing how you and others feel and whether these emotions are helpful or not, you can leverage the power of emotions to successfully lead others and your organization through change. Over the long haul, a positive emotional climate leads to better outcomes. But sadness, anger and anxiety have tactical, short-term advantages and the emotionally intelligent leader must know how to leverage all emotions.

Emotional Intelligence—Definition and Origin

Emotional intelligence means different things to different people. Emotional intelligence became part of our culture in 1995 when Daniel Goleman[4] wrote a book on emotional intelligence that started a worldwide conversation. He is rightly credited for bringing emotional intelligence into the spotlight. As a scientific theory, however, emotional intelligence was first written about in a 1990 paper by John "Jack" Mayer and Peter Salovey[5] who defined emotional intelligence as: "The ability to monitor one's own and other's feelings and emotions, to discriminate among them, and to use this infor-

---

3   We suggest a great book on how positive psychology has gone wrong: Ehrenreich, B. (2009). *Bright-Sided: How Positive Thinking Is Undermining America*. New York: Henry Holt.
4   Goleman, D. (1995.) Emotional Intelligence. NY: Bantam Books.
5   Salovey, P. & Mayer, J. D. (1990). Emotional intelligence. Imagination, Cognition, and Personality, 9, 185-211.

mation to guide one's thinking and action".[6] Jack is now a professor of psychology at the University of New Hampshire and Peter Salovey is the president of Yale University. This definition of emotional intelligence differs greatly from other definitions. In this approach emotions can be smart, emotional intelligence is a form of intelligence and it's also a set of "hard" rather than "soft" skills.

In 1996, David Caruso joined Jack and Peter to begin to create an ability-based test, like an IQ test, that measures a person's ability to perceive, use, understand and manage emotions. After several years, they created the Mayer, Salovey, Caruso Emotional Intelligence Test (MSCEIT) which measures a person's emotional intelligence and helps them leverage their strengths and become aware of areas they may want to develop[7]. This guide is based on the work of Jack and Peter and incorporates research based on the MSCEIT.

Whether you have assessed your EI skills objectively or not, you can use this guide to leverage skills you possess or enhance those that are less developed. Our guide is designed for busy leaders who know the importance of emotions in the workplace and want useful tips on how to strengthen their skills using real life examples. By the end of this guide, and with a little practice, you can harness the power of emotions and transition from a good leader to a great leader. Frankly, it's not all that difficult, but what is extremely challenging is deploying these skills on a consistent and effective basis. We've met a few people—out of thousands—who can do this. That means most of us need to work hard to develop these skills.

---

6   If Daniel Goleman did not write his book in 1995 few people would ever have heard of emotional intelligence. While our approach differs from his, it is important to recognize that his book has made our work visible and possible.

7   Mayer, J., Salovey, P, & Caruso, D. (2002). The Mayer, Salovey Caruso Emotional Intelligence Test. Toronto: MHS.

Using Emotional Intelligence Skills on a Broader Scale

For us, the world changed dramatically in early 2020 due to the pandemic. What we foolishly and naively did not realize until recently, is that the world was already an unwelcoming and unsafe place for many of our friends, colleagues, customers, students and leaders. The two of us, as white authors, have a point of view and a set of experiences in the world which may differ from those of some of our readers and we recognize and acknowledge our limited viewpoint. It is our hope, again probably naïve, that the skills of emotional intelligence, especially being able to recognize and then to feel and understand what other people experience, may help us to create more just and equitable organizations and eventually, societies. We also believe that it takes moral courage and emotional resilience to engage in this work, and again, it is our hope that by adopting some of the Move emotions strategies, you will be able to stay strong and enhance your well-being so you can engage in the struggle.

PART ONE

THE EMOTIONAL INTELLIGENCE FRAMEWORK

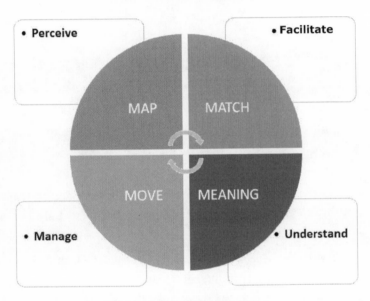

Figure 1: The EI Ability Model

THE FRAMEWORK OF EMOTIONAL INTELLIGENCE IS SIMple and contains 4 abilities—the ability to Perceive, Use, Understand and Manage emotions. Each ability has its own characteristics and all work together to form emotional intelligence. We use the more memorable labels of *Map* (Perceive), *Match* (Facilitate), *Meaning* (Understand) and *Move* (Manage), for better retention[8].

---

8   "Use" is sometimes called "Facilitation" or "Facilitation of Thought".

You may wonder where things like optimism, happiness or assertiveness are in this model. Our approach to emotional intelligence—sometimes called the ability model of EI—consists of a set of hard skills or abilities. In this approach, EI is an intelligence, related to other intelligences. There is nothing wrong or unimportant about optimism, but it is a traditional personality trait and is not a skill nor is it part of emotional intelligence, at least in our view.

The Business Case for Emotional Intelligence

You may have heard emotional intelligence is critically important to achieving "success". While it can help in certain ways, we'd suggest first hiring smart and conscientious people to fill executive roles. These characteristics can't be developed. If your newly-hired Chief Operating Officer lacks emotional intelligence, for example, we can help them acquire those skills[9].

Why, then, does emotional intelligence matter at work? If you read through the research, and read the research on the ability model, you will discover that EI predicts certain outcomes. It's not as important in transactions—scripted interactions between people. But it is a good predictor of the quality of long-term relationships. EI, ability EI, is a good predictor of "what" a leader achieves but is a better predictor of "how" a leader achieves their goals. These results suggest that the emotionally intelligent leader can hit their targets while still acting with integrity. That's important because it's not just

---

9   Note that we do not claim that EI can be increased, per se. We are claiming that you can develop remedial or compensatory strategies.

about being "nice", it is about results. Resilience and success-fully coping with stress are also outcomes of higher EI[10].

Map (Perceive) Emotions

Emotions contain data. You make decisions based on data—reports, analyses, surveys, policies, etc. When was the last time you made an important decision based on emotions? The answer should be "every single decision", or perhaps more accurately, "every single good decision". We are taught to keep emotions out of it but emotions impact everything we do whether we realize it or not. Sometimes, emotions help us make great decisions—if we leverage the skills of EI—but at other times emotions trip us up because we fail to accurately read the situation.

Think of your typical work day. What emotions do you feel and see in the workplace? And what impact are these emotions having on your ability to lead? Chances are you experience emotions constantly, but are you paying atten-tion to them? Perhaps you feel that emotions aren't relevant in the workplace—but you may want to think again. Take a moment to recall a recent meeting you led where you had a very specific goal in mind. You began the meeting plowing through the agenda and then something happened. Someone became upset. Perhaps they became angry and started to

---

10   See, for example, Mayer, J.D., Caruso, D.R., & Salovey, P. (2016). The ability model of emotional intelligence: Principles and updates. *Emotion Review*, 8, 1-11. Mayer, J. D., Salovey, P., & Caruso, D.R. (2012). The validity of the MSCEIT: additional analyses and evidence. *Emotion Review*. 4, 1-6. Mayer, J. D., Salovey, P., & Caruso, D.R. (2008). Emotion-al Intelligence: New Ability or Eclectic Mix of Traits? *American Psychol-ogist, 63,* 503-517.

raise their voice. Perhaps someone began to cry or became despondent. Or perhaps there was complete silence as people looked down at the conference room table. You found yourself surprised and confused by the reactions of your team, and the goal you had at the beginning of the meeting is now a distant memory. Unfortunately, this happens more than it should. That is why the first part of emotional intelligence is accurately identifying how people are feeling before moving further into the discussion.

How do you know how people are feeling? Chances are if you asked anyone how they are feeling they would say something like—"fine", "good" or "ok". Unfortunately, these answers are not very helpful in accurately identifying someone's emotions—the polite responses, so commonplace in today's society, are almost completely without meaning. In all likelihood, when we ask "how are you?", we do so to be polite, not to get an honest answer! Sheryl Sandberg, in her book written with Adam Grant, *Option B*[11], tells the story of how people asked "how are you?" right after her husband died and likely expected the typical non-answer.

One way to really know how someone is feeling is by using our Mood Map (Figure 2). Emotions can be measured on two axes—by the level of energy and the level of pleasantness. If someone has high energy and high pleasantness, they are feeling happiness and joy. If they are experiencing high energy and low pleasantness, then chances are they are feeling angry, frustrated or overwhelmed. If they are feeling low energy and low pleasantness then they may be experiencing boredom or sadness. And finally, if they are experiencing low energy and high pleasantness, they are most likely feeling content.

---

11   Sandberg, S. & Grant, A. (2017). *Option B*. NY: Knopf. They cite David in their book.

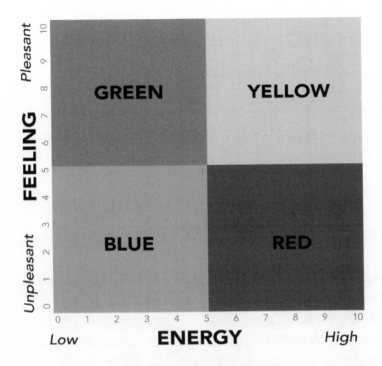

Figure 2: The Mood Map

Asking someone their energy level and how pleasant they are feeling is a quick and easy way for determining someone's emotional state, though it may not be practical and seem a little odd in some work contexts. So, here are some tips you can use to get better at assessing someone's emotions.

Helpful Questions to Map Emotions

- ✓ Context—is the person acting differently than they normally do?
- ✓ Body language—what are their posture and movements telling me?

✓ Tone of voice—do their words match the tone of their voice?

✓ Silence—are they communicating effectively or have they shut down?

Application

Here are some ideas to help you apply this skill.

A. How to ask, "How are you?"

You should find your own questions but try the ones below as a start.

✓ How you ask matters: Ask in a tone that invites a real, honest response.

✓ How has your day been so far?

✓ Tell me what's going on?

✓ What are your thoughts about _____?

✓ On a scale of 1 to 10 .... How do you feel about ___?

✓ How do you feel about this on a scale of 1 to 10 ... What would get you to a 10?

✓ What is on your mind?

✓ You seem ___. Is that right? (Low energy can be seen as low interest rather than being reflective.)

Culture is critical. All cultures have what are called "display rules". "Culture" in this context refers to your organization, your family, your country of origin or the specific department you work in. Every organization has its own display rules and these rules determine which emotions can be shown and when and how they can be shown. In many situations, our felt emotions do not match our expressed emotions. Know your culture to ask a question that will generate an honest answer. Know when, when not and how to ask "how are you?"

B. Map Emotions Checklist

- ✓ Check in with yourself—how are you feeling?
- ✓ Before beginning an important conversation, identify the emotional state of the other person/s.
- ✓ What is the emotional environment (vibe) in the room?
- ✓ How are people feeling during the discussion?
- ✓ Are you getting the results you desire?

C. Warnings and What to Watch For

- ✓ Be hyper-aware of when you ask the "how are you" question and allow people to pass. You have a position of power over employees and others, and you cannot, even unintentionally, abuse this power.
- ✓ There are data on cross-cultural emotion perception inaccuracies. You must exercise even greater caution when mapping the emotions of diverse groups of people, especially those who differ from you in terms of various identities.

INTERESTING FACT: Each of us has a different "neutral" emotional facial expression. It's very difficult to know what your resting emotional expression looks like to others unless you yourself can see it. Use a mirror, or take selfies or, even better, use your webcam as you work and video yourself over the course of routine tasks. Then play it back and see what you think.

Match (Facilitate) Emotions

Accurately mapping emotions, knowing what emotions you and others are experiencing, is the critical start to emotional intelligence. The next step is determining whether these emotions will help you reach your shared goal. We call this—matching the mood to the task at hand.

Let's go back to the Mood Map (Figure 3) and overlay it with the emotions for each of the four quadrants and how these emotions can be useful depending on the situation. For example, you are about to go into a meeting with your team to discuss an important project that is falling behind schedule. Before the meeting you are feeling worried, frustrated and a little overwhelmed. You know your emotions are contagious and your current emotional state won't be helpful to your team. Remembering that emotions direct your thinking and influence your behavior you ask yourself—what emotions will help my team have a successful meeting?

Some people feel there are good and bad emotions—but in reality, all emotions serve a constructive purpose. Typically, anger is displayed when there is injustice, inequity or a dream not realized. Anger can and does drive positive growth and change: think of The Equal Rights Movement and the ongoing fight for women's equality. Sadness is felt when there is loss, happiness when something is gained and fear when people feel threatened. We have spent a good deal of time and effort working through how to share the importance and helpful nature of all emotions. As we noted earlier, this is not a book about happiness or positive psychology and to us, some of that work seems to focus purely on your own happiness and encourages you to filter out "negative" experiences or emotions. That's not smart and it's not what good leaders should do. Life is difficult and filled with stressors and challenges. Emotions—anger, sadness, happiness—provide us with different perspectives on problems and are all necessary to engage with to be an effective leader. The key is to match the emotion to the task. We know based on research that some emotions are more helpful than others depending on the situation. Therefore, the next time you are about to go into a meeting, determine what emotions are the most helpful to achieve your goal.

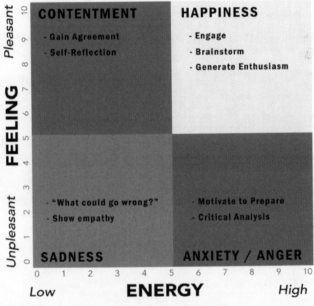

Figure 3: Map then Match

Emotions are also used to connect with people. Think of someone in your life who mentored you, gave you great advice or inspired you to be your best. Chances are they connected with you emotionally. We use emotions to show empathy, care and concern for others. Successful leaders understand the importance of emotions to build meaningful relationships and understand how they can inspire and motivate others. More than that, great leaders create an emotional climate that allows people to get the job done. Sometimes, that means lighting a fire under people to create a sense of urgency. There can be a downside to feeling what others feel. Emotional empathy, this feelings-based connection with others, can take a toll on you. If you feel what others feel it can be draining. Psychologist Paul Bloom has a well-reasoned argument against emotional empathy[12], instead suggesting that cognitive empathy (rational compassion) might be more effective. But rather than feeling less, what if we managed those feelings better? To us, that seems like a better solution than closing yourself off to the emotional world of others, although at times that would seem the emotionally safest course. To do so habitually is to avoid confronting important challenges: personal, family, work, and societal.

We want to caution you—while *all* emotions can be smart (including anger, anxiety, and sadness)—we are not giving you license to act like a jerk. We explain more about expressing and moving emotions later, but you need to tread with great care around these powerful emotions. Effectively moving emotions to lead change cannot be about you. You cannot act in an angry manner, but you can allow anger to fuel change if, and only if, you have the emotion management expertise to harness its energy. Remember, over the long-term, great leaders create a positive and supportive climate—the kind of environment where people bring their "A" game every day.

When fueling change, consider anger as raw energy, like a barrel of jet fuel. If you aren't careful and unwittingly toss a match into that barrel it blows up in your face. Anger has a

---

12   Bloom, P. (2016). *Against Empathy: The Case for Rational Compassion*. NY: Ecco.

bad reputation, because people with lower EI try to harness the raw energy of anger and end up destroying themselves and others. However, people possessing finely-developed EI skills can take the same anger, the barrel of fuel, and harness it like a highly-sophisticated and engineered jet engine takes the jet fuel and uses it to power flight. (See Figure 4.)

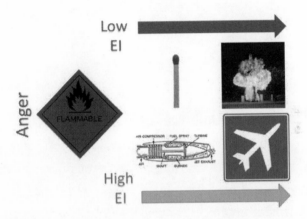

Figure 4. The Destructive and Constructive Power of Anger

Before you try to harness your own anger to affect the greater good, ask yourself whether you are ready for the consequences. Be certain you possess the skills necessary to channel that anger into a constructive process. Master the ability to effectively manage emotions, otherwise it's going to blow up in your face.

Helpful Questions for Matching Emotions

✓ What emotions are we feeling?

✓ Are these emotions helpful to reach the goal? (Use Fig. 3.)

✓ Am I using emotions to connect with others?

✓ Do I regularly engage with others' emotions?

Here are some ideas to help you apply this skill.

A. Matching Mood to the Task at Hand

✓ What tasks do we do on a recurring basis?

✓ What emotions do we typically feel when we do these tasks?

✓ Are these emotions helpful to the task?

✓ What emotions would be more helpful?

✓ How can we generate a morse helpful emotion before or during the task?

B. Matching Emotions Checklist

✓ Each day look for opportunities to connect with others

✓ Is there someone who needs your attention? Is someone displaying sadness, boredom, anger, frustration, etc.?

✓ Create a safe environment for a meaningful conversation that is confidential, non-judgmental, with no retribution

✓ Practice deep meaning in the words said and not said, body language (although this is extremely difficult to do well) and emotions

✓ Seek to understand their point of view—what's going on for them, what are they concerned about, and how can you help (maybe it's helping by just listening)

C. Warnings and What to Watch For

✓ Make sure you, your employees or colleagues have the skill to move and manage emotions that are generated when developing your Match emotions skills. It is unfair to push emotions onto others, especially if they are not ready or prepared to experience those emotions.

✓ "I know how you feel" – we hear this often, but we can never truly feel what others feel, we can only approximate their lived experience. Don't say to someone "I know how you feel." Instead, consider reflecting their feelings and physical sensations through your unambiguous non-verbal signals and some general, verbal statements. For example, an obvious smile combined with a clear "Wow! That sounds really exciting!" can send the message.

✓ The skills of EI need to be matched with cultural competence. Even the most empathetic person cannot begin to accurately "get" the emotional experience of another person if they lack this competence. Do not assume others' reactions to events are similar to yours. Do not assume you know how someone else feels. This skill, in the absence of cultural awareness and competence, can do great harm because you will assume a shared feeling when it does not exist.

✓ Develop your Move skills, discussed later in the book, before enhancing your emotional empathy.

INTERESTING FACT: Not convinced of the importance of emotions such as sadness and anger? You can read the research. Or, you can watch the Pixar animated movie *Inside Out*! Two emotions researchers consulted on the movie and the data behind it are very solid.

Meaning of (Understand) Emotions

After accurately identifying emotions (Map) and determining which emotion would be more helpful to achieve the goal (Match), we need to understand why we feel the way we do and how emotions can shift and change over time (Meaning).

We are now seeking to understand what caused the emotion in the first place. You must understand the root cause of the emotion to know what it means—whether it represents actionable data or not. Leaders frequently make the mistake of hypothesizing the reason behind others' emotions, or avoid them entirely because knowing the reason can be uncomfortable. Instead of avoiding emotions, get curious. Take time to think about the person—what emotions are they experiencing, what might be the cause for their emotion and how can you help move them to a better place?

Take a moment to think of the people you rely on for your success. Perhaps it's your boss, your family, your colleagues and of course, your employees. Now ask yourself—what makes this person "tick"? Meaning, do you know what makes them happy, sad, bored, excited, frustrated, proud, disgusted and angry? To communicate and collaborate effectively with others you need to know them really well. And you need to meet them where they are—instead of following the golden rule of treating them as *you* would want to be treated, follow the platinum rule—treat them as *they* want to be treated.

Getting to know what makes people tick takes time and practice. Some people will make it easy for you and share their emotions, interests and passions, while others will not, depending on their personality, culture, life experiences and comfort level with sharing this type of information— especially with their boss. However, by demonstrating your understanding of others, you can really connect with them to move them towards where they need to be to reach the collective goal.

Understand What Makes People Tick

As mentioned earlier, some people will tell you exactly how they're feeling and why they feel the way they do. Others will challenge you to figure out what's going on with them.

To understand others, they need to trust your intentions. Letting them know why you want to get to know them better helps—share that you want to be a better boss/colleague, you want to know what is important to them. You don't have to get personal, you can start with work (see Table 1). Asking them questions such as—What do you like most about your work? What frustrates you at work? What makes you bored? What fires you up? What do you look forward to? Once you begin this conversation you may be surprised where it leads. Next, be attentive when they express emotion at work—what emotion did you see? What was the cause? You begin to get an idea of what makes the person tick without even asking.

EMOTION	GENERAL CAUSE	APPLICATION	EXAMPLE
Frustration	What aspect of the work frustrates you?	Avoid annoying one another	*Provide a safe environment to share concerns*
Boredom	What tasks do you find dull?	Assign and reassign tasks	*Empower employee to find new ways for doing mundane work*
Happiness	What type of work do you enjoy?	Align work to employee's strengths	*Find opportunities to showcase strengths more*

EMOTION	GENERAL CAUSE	APPLICATION	EXAMPLE
Pride	What accomplishments at work are you most proud of?	Understand how to motivate	*Tailor recognition to the person— formal, informal, or a simple thank you*

Table 1: Understanding Emotions at Work

Use Your Words!

The emotionally intelligent leader uses words carefully. Don't just toss out any word: select the best emotion word to convey meaning, to get people's attention and to help them understand the situation. Don't say you are enraged if you are merely annoyed—that only confuses people. If you go to red alert all the time, your staff will avoid you and you may lose credibility. Conversely, if you have been promised the quarterly sales forecasts for days and your staff fails to deliver, you can legitimately say you are disappointed and quite annoyed. One of the advantages of building your emotion vocabulary is that you will be a better communicator. One key is to deliver these emotion words after Moving your emotions (see below) to a more neutral state on the Mood Map. Otherwise, you risk being seen as "too emotional" or the energy of your expression can cause people to become defensive. Table 2 adds helpful emotion words for you to use to better communicate exactly how you are feeling. (For a longer list of words see our workbook, *Developing Your Emotional Intelligence Skills*.)

EMOTION	GENERAL CAUSE	WORDS
Frustration	Blocked from getting something you want and value.	Irritated Annoyed Frustrated Angry Enraged
Disgust	Your values are violated or offended.	Distasteful Objectionable Disgusted Loathsome
Happiness	Gain something you value.	Contented Pleased Happy Delighted Joyous
Worry	Possible threat.	Concerned Worried Anxious Afraid Terror
Surprise	Something unexpected.	Distracted Interested Surprised Amazed Shocked
Sadness	Lose something you value.	Pensive Disappointed Sad Miserable Depressed

Table 2: Emotion Words at Work

To understand emotions, it helps to build your emotional vocabulary and understand how emotions progress and blend to form more complex emotions. One of the easiest ways to do this is by studying our simple illustration of emotions (Figure 5).

Figure 5: Emotion Wheel

You may be familiar with all the emotions listed in the Wheel but only identify with emotions that are universal—happiness, sadness, fear, surprise, disgust and anger. (If you are interested in a beautiful mathematical representation of emotions, search for "Plutchik Emotion Circumplex", an interesting illustration of how emotions progress.) For example, annoyance, when left unattended can lead to anger, which can then lead to rage. Boredom can lead to disgust which can lead to loathing. Therefore, it is critical to identify emotion, especially negative emotion, early so that it doesn't progress into something that could have an unintended impact on your organization.

Not only do emotions progress, they also blend to form more complex emotions. The emotions of joy and trust blend to become love, and disgust and anger blend to become contempt. Emotions have many nuances and are often mislabeled. Many people say they are angry when they are frustrated (milder emotion). Or they say they love everything, when they are only interested (mild). The more accurate we are at naming emotions, the better we can uncover the cause of the emotion and how to move it in a more helpful direction. A sophisticated, precise emotion vocabulary helps us and others better understand and communicate more accurately and efficiently.

Feelings, Moods, Emotions

Understanding emotions can be confusing because we use the words feelings, moods and emotions interchangeably—even in this guide. To get better at understanding feelings remember this: a mood is something that is general, diffuse and often unclear. For example, we woke up on the "wrong side of the bed" and are in a foul mood. We try to understand why we feel the way we do, but we just can't, or we realize, "I am just feeling cranky today". Therefore, it's important to move the mood (which we'll discuss in the next section of this guide). However, if upon examining how we feel there is a source, this is data we can then use to make better decisions. In short, you should attend to the feeling you have, but analyze its source. If it's a mood, Move it; if it's an emotion, Match it. Figure 6 shows you a Feelings decision tree.

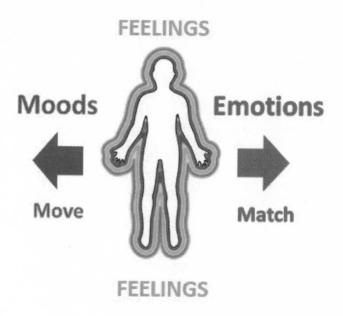

Figure 6. Feelings Are Not Always Facts

Helpful Questions for Making Meaning of Emotions

- ✓ Am I developing and enhancing my emotion vocabulary to better communicate ideas?
- ✓ Who do I rely on for my success?
- ✓ Do I know what makes this person tick?
- ✓ Do I understand why they feel the way they do?
- ✓ Do I know how to move them to a place they need to be to reach their goal?
- ✓ Do I understand why I feel the way I do? Is it a mood (move it) or is it an emotion (data) that I should be paying attention to?

✓ Do I share with people what makes me tick so they can communicate with me more effectively?

✓ Remember—feelings are not always facts: moods can be wrong, but emotions are data.

Application

Here are some ideas to help you apply this skill.

A. Emotional What-If?

✓ Before your next meeting conduct an emotional "what-if" analysis: what could possibly happen?

✓ What is the goal of my meeting?

✓ What is the best time and place for this meeting to take place to ensure we are at our best?

✓ Knowing the other person as well as I do, how might the person react to what I need to tell them?

✓ What questions will I ask, what tone of voice should I use, what is the best body language?

✓ If they react negatively, what can I do to keep the conversation going in a positive direction? If they react positively, how do I acknowledge or "capitalize" on that for the goals set out.

✓ Can I show more empathy, listen more, seek a common goal?

B. Meaning of Emotions Checklist

✓ Consider the source of your feelings

✓ Do not act on a feeling until you truly understand its source

✓ Review the day, your feelings and consider how much of the feeling is due to a mood and how much to an emotion

✓ Ask yourself whether someone else would feel the same way and whether the feeling is reasonable

✓ If the feeling is mostly a mood—ignore and move it (see Move section)

✓ If the feeling is mostly an emotion—attend to it and act on it

B. Warnings and What to Watch For

✓ Do not ask someone for their emotion causes unless you will, 1) remember what the person tells you, and 2) employ this knowledge to strengthen the relationship. In other words, if you signal you care about someone and do not follow through, it can be hurtful.

✓ When you do forget an individual's unique emotion cause, note it and apologize.

✓ You need to apply this skill through the lens of cultural competence and examine the various social and cultural identities of oneself and others, understand and appreciate diversity from a historically grounded and strengths-focused lens." If you fail to take the perspective of others, you will appear to lack cognitive empathy, you will not be able to "get" someone else and worse, you will think you have.

✓ As always, watch the power dynamic of a leader asking an employee for their emotion causes. Mutual sharing is one way to reduce the possible misuse of this strategy, but please be careful and vigilant to not abuse the technique.

INTERESTING FACT: Leaders often understand the importance of getting to know their employees but few share with them what makes them "tick". If you don't share what makes you happy, proud, frustrated or angry, then you are setting the relationship up for failure. How will your employees know what to do more or less of if you don't let them know?

Move (Manage) Emotions

The last step in the EI framework is moving emotions. It is the easiest ability to grasp, and the most difficult to execute. The prior three abilities of Map, Match and Meaning can be performed perfectly, but moving your emotion, and those of others, will determine if you behave as an emotionally intelligent leader. You are judged in your interactions with others, so it's critical to get proficient at both moving your emotions and those around you.

The first step in moving your emotions, especially strong ones, is to be aware of how emotions show up in your body. Many people feel anger in their chest, throat or jaw. Some feel fear when they get goosebumps or the hair raises on the back of their neck. Joy is frequently experienced with a lightness in their body and warmth in their heart. For each person it is different. Ask yourself, where do emotions typically show up in my body? By being aware, you can react appropriately when your body sends you a sign. This ability is critical and takes practice because unanalyzed feelings leads us to make terrible decisions or to say things we regret in the heat of the moment. However, listening to our body allows our brain to catch up with the emotion, to fully process why we feel the way we do and to remind us of the goal we want to achieve so we make the best decision regardless of our emotional state.

In business, we are often told to suppress our emotions, and as leaders we keep tamping them down. We pride ourselves on being the calm in the storm, for not showing emotions, for holding everything in despite how we feel. But at some level, we know this behavior is not sustainable or recommended. If you suppress emotions too long they may come out in inappropriate ways and have unintended consequences. Eventually, suppressed anger may lead to destructive rage and devastating results. And bottling up emotions makes you appear fake, inauthentic or uncaring. Bottom line, suppressing emotion is unhealthy for everyone and eventually erodes trust.

The best strategies for moving emotions are the long-term ones—getting adequate sleep, eating the right foods, getting enough exercise, seeking social support, prayer, meditation and making time for relaxation. We know long-term strategies are what we should be doing, but we often don't do what's best for us. So, what else can you do to effectively move emotions? Depending on the situation, you may choose either strategic or responsive approaches—or both. Think of a time when you were in a meeting and someone or something got you really annoyed. Chances are you felt it—perhaps a tightness in your chest or you felt hot in the face. Everyone is looking at you to see how you are going to respond. This is where the rubber hits the road—what strategy are you going to use to reach your collective goal? How will you say it? What tone of voice? How will you keep the meeting on track?

Moving emotions doesn't only include you. By behaving in an emotionally intelligent manner you are also able to move other people's emotions. This concept may seem odd because you're probably thinking you don't have control over the emotions of others and that is true. However, your response to other's emotions can greatly impact the effectiveness of the conversation. For example, let's say you are giving an employee some critical feedback and they start to become angry and yell or perhaps they become sad and begin to cry. There are many strategies you can use to continue the dialogue—showing empathy, listening, seeking understanding, being supportive, showing care, working towards a common goal, etc.

The key to helping others move their emotions is to move your own during the conversation—leading by example. How can you remain neutral or, at times, generate a positive state? (It's okay, and can be very intelligent to be angry, but it is rarely a good idea to act aggressively.) How can you establish an environment for others to share what is important to them? How can you show empathy while still reaching your collective goal? How can you "light a fire" under an unmotivated employee? Moving emotions successfully takes practice, but if you stay open to all types of emotion, you will be better able to connect and communicate with others. Below (Table 3) is a list of effective (and easy) strategies for moving *your* emotions.

STRATEGY	EXAMPLE
Prepare	Do a quick run-through of possible outcomes, not just desired or expected outcomes. For example, ask yourself, "Is it possible my new employee will become defensive when I give them feedback?"
Modify Mood	If you know your emotion isn't helpful to your goal—change it! Psych yourself up before a big meeting. Or calm yourself down if you need to get your "gameface" on.
Reappraise	Don't fall for first impressions. We all act badly at times, but few of us are real jerks. Consider whether the other person is just having a bad day.

STRATEGY	EXAMPLE
Self-talk	Use your inner voice. Repeat some calming or motivational thoughts to get through stressful moments.
Physiological	Take a deep breath, take a walk or a break, smile.
Intervening Moment	Take a moment to think. Remember your goal. Look down. Count to ten. Take a deep breath. Write it down but don't share. Go for a walk. Take a break. When really bothered just say "let me get back to you".
Express a Different Emotion	If you cannot change the time of a meeting or the situation, and the show must go on, express the desired emotion. It's not suppressing, it is expressing and generating a more helpful emotion.
Long Term	Get adequate sleep, eat a healthy diet, meditate, have fun, pray, seek social support, get some exercise (especially with others).
Relationships	Although this is also a long-term strategy it's important enough to list on its own. Cherish your family, friends and cultivate good colleagues. And be a good friend and colleague to others. Strong social networks are vital to our long-term emotional health.

Table 3. Emotion Management Strategies—You

Once you deploy effective emotion management strategies, you begin to improve your ability to move other people's emotions. Moving emotions is not manipulative—if you connect with other people and feel for them, you will "do the right thing". We've listed strategies you can try with other people in Table 4. You will invariably make mistakes when practicing this ability so be ready with one of the best emotion management strategies in the world: a heartfelt apology.

STRATEGY	EXAMPLE
Distraction	Change the subject. "Hey, let's grab a cup of coffee". Use this strategy sparingly, otherwise you will never successfully manage the underlying issues!
Select or Modify Situation	Meet when you're at your best. "Monday's are really hectic so let's have our weekly review meeting on Tuesday mornings."
Change Situation	Take a time out. "I need to think about this for a few minutes. Let's come back in 5 minutes and when we do, I'd like to move on to the second topic ..."
Emotional Connection	Show you care. "That sounds difficult. How can I help?" "Is there anything I can do?"
Match and Validate	Don't argue, instead validate the person's perspective and feelings. "I can see how you might feel that way."

STRATEGY	EXAMPLE
Modulate Tone	Change it up and get their attention. Increase or decrease the volume and pitch of your speech to either calm things down or energize the other person.
Physiological Techniques	Have walking meetings, lunch meetings, take breaks. Stand up every now and then.

Table 4. Emotion Management Strategies—Others

It's Not All About Your Being Positive and Relaxed

Recall the lessons and tips from Matching Emotions that all emotions can be smart. The goal of emotion management is not to relax and engage in positive emotions all of the time. The emphasis on "self-care" in some cases and at some times can lull us into complacency. The goal of moving emotions is not a single-minded focus on your well-being. Some people suggest you do things like disengage from reading the latest news in order to maintain your peaceful tranquility. We recognize your life is filled with stress and there are times when you need to turn off and disconnect (we do support turning your phone off, for example!). But at the same time, many people do not have the luxury (privilege) of not thinking about the latest headlines because they live these headlines everyday. Our goal is not to have you be a happy, upbeat, cheery, positive person all of the time. We want you to engage with and grapple with the toughest leadership challenges and to succeed at those challenges. We want you, in short, to change the world and make it a better place to live. At the same time we urge you to fill up your emotional reserves. The goal is not to keep a smile on your face and be happy—it is to give you the skills, focus and energy so you have the emotion resources to engage with the toughest leadership challenges. You need to be at your best if you are engaging in the struggle to create change and to drive innovation in your organization. Another benefit of these management strategies is you will not always bring your work home with you—we want you to be emotionally available to your family and friends.

Helpful Questions for Moving Emotions:

- ✓ Am I getting enough sleep, exercise, good food, relaxation, social support?
- ✓ Do I recognize where emotions show up in my body?
- ✓ Before reacting, do I take time to think about my response? What is my goal? How do I keep things moving in a positive direction?
- ✓ Do I stay open to other people's feelings? Do I show empathy? Do I try to understand their point of view? Do I listen? Do I support them while still holding them accountable?
- ✓ Do I show my emotions genuinely?
- ✓ Do I use my emotions to inspire, motivate, communicate and connect to others?

Application

Here are some ideas on how to apply these skills.

A. Filling Up Your Emotional Reserve

To give your best, you must be at your best, which means taking care of yourself to have the energy to fully tackle your challenges.

✓ Take a moment to think of those activities, that when you do them, you are completely fulfilled, happy, peaceful, re-energized or relaxed.

✓ On a blank piece of paper, write these activities until you can't think of anything else to add.

✓ Now review the list and circle three activities that you will commit to doing in the next week.

✓ Try to do at least three activities a week for at least a month. Better yet—find someone who will help you stay committed to these activities or will do some of them with you!

B. Moving Others' Emotions Checklist

✓ Have you created a safe environment for others?

✓ What are the emotions that you are seeing and sensing?

✓ Are these emotions helpful in the situation?

✓ Is your emotional state helpful?

✓ If not, what emotional management responsive or compensating strategies will you use?

C. Move Anxiety and Anger Checklist

✓ If anger or anxiety are the ideal emotions for the task, you can only leverage them if you have Olympic-level emotion management skills.

✓ Check to make sure the anger really is justified— make sure it's not just a mood and make sure it's not personal.

✓ Use any and all of the self-management strategies.

✓ Reconsider the underlying causes of your anger in a calmer state: would someone else feel the same way for example?

✓ Practice a scenario in your head where you explain the frustration to others and consider multiple "what-if" analyses to determine the best way to get the message through.

✓ Ask yourself—is it worth it? Will showing negative emotions damage the relationship I've tried so hard to establish?

✓ The message will only get through if people are not attacked.

✓ Now, in that calm and focused state—where you can accurately Map, Match, and understand the Meaning of emotions—express your frustration using emotion words.

D. Warnings and What to Watch For

✓ Leaders experience high levels of burnout and stress, thus the need for these self-focused emotion management strategies.

✓ However, many leaders experience dissatisfaction with their position due to external factors such as the global market, environmental conditions, and political dynamics. These factors can be demoralizing, which differs from burnout. Demoralization requires systemic change; it is not something you can meditate your way out of.

✓ Even those with high levels of emotional intelligence will not be able to successfully Move emotions all the time. Expect setbacks – practice these skills, seek feedback, tweak your approach, and try again.

✓ Remember it is okay to suppress emotions at times! In fact, sometimes silence is golden and is the best and most appropriate strategy.

✓ Leaders do not practice on your employees! You have to apply these techniques and skills with care and at a high level of proficiency. Start with peers, get feedback, refine your approach, and then deploy these strategies more broadly.

INTERESTING FACT: Many leaders feel they are experts at suppressing their emotion and think they have a "poker face". Unfortunately, that isn't the case. Emotions—especially anger, frustration and surprise—are difficult to disguise well. And even if you are good at it, if you didn't show emotion in certain situations, your employees might feel that the issue isn't important or you don't care what happens.

Putting It All Together (The EI Blueprint)

Congratulations! You've learned the 4 abilities of emotional intelligence and now comes the fun part—putting it all together to be an emotionally intelligent leader. In summary, everything you have learned in this guide works together seamlessly as outlined in the EI Blueprint below (Figure 7).

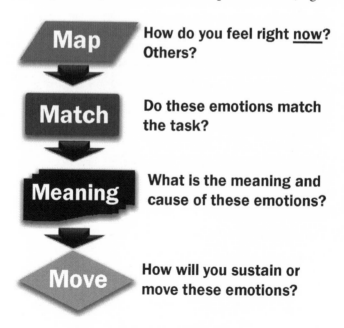

Figure 7. EI Blueprint

The Blueprint is a simple tool in principle, but like most simple ideas, it's difficult to apply well and consistently. Below is a common work situation leaders face on a recurring basis and how you can use the EI Blueprint to achieve positive results.

Emotional Blueprint Example: *Providing Critical Feedback*[13]

BACKGROUND Joe has been with the company for two years and thinks he is indispensable to the organization. He constantly seeks praise, doesn't work well with others and is always looking for a better job but has yet to find one. Historically, his work is average but he is starting to act out in meetings and his work isn't getting done on time with the level of quality you expect from your team. As his boss, you know it's time for a conversation to discuss the situation.

GOAL Joe is a good employee who could be a great employee. My goal is to understand the reasons for his behavior, to provide him with candid feedback and to help him reach his career and our organizational goals.

Using the EI Blueprint

- **MAP EMOTIONS**
  What are the emotions—yours and others?
  ✓ I am feeling *frustrated* and *annoyed* with Joe. I have bent over backwards trying to give him advice and it is falling on deaf ears. I believe that Joe feels *frustrated*

---

13   Every case study disguises the identity of the leader and organization. We do not use actual names and change details of the case such as the industry.

and perhaps *disappointed* that he hasn't been promoted. He probably thinks that I don't value his work or care about him.

- **MATCH EMOTIONS**

  What emotions are most helpful?

  ✓ My frustration is not helpful to the conversation. I need to remember Joe is passionate about his work, he wants to do a good job and he wants recognition. Joe's recent behavior of avoiding his team, being abrupt, not sharing important information, missing deadlines and showing his aggravation in the workplace is having a negative impact on those around him. I want to move him from frustration to a more neutral state so he is not defensive and is open to having an honest discussion.

- **MEANING OF EMOTIONS**

  What is the cause of these emotions?

  ✓ I have tried giving Joe advice many times and he isn't listening to me. I am getting really frustrated by his behavior and part of me doesn't want to even bother. However, I haven't been able to spend much time with Joe lately. I know Joe has been under a lot of pressure both in and out of the office. He is a new parent and the sole breadwinner for his family. Even "happy" events are stressful and perhaps he is feeling overwhelmed (and exhausted).

- **MOVE EMOTIONS**

  How will you sustain or move these emotions?

  ✓ During the meeting I will make sure to ask about the baby, his work goals, ask him what he wants out of his career and ask him if he is open to hearing feedback. I will ask him how I can better support reaching his goals. I find his emotions hard to handle and sometimes I take them personally. Instead of allowing his feelings to overwhelm me, I will stay open to his emotions, ask him questions to gain understanding, show empathy, ask his opinion, share with him my goals and how I am here to support him. How? I'll practice scenarios where this happens, take a deep breath, and have some phrases ready such as "I can see how you feel that way" and "How can I help you?" Joe can be very emotional going from anger to sadness and even joy in one conversation. If he begins to get angry and loses focus, I'll try a different question. I'll remind him of the goal for our conversation—that I am here to support him. I will practice deep listening and try to understand his perspective. If the conversation begins to go badly, we will take a break and re-engage on a different agenda item.

STRATEGIES USED Modify Mood; Reappraise; Physiological; Emotional Connection; Match and Validate.

OUTCOME Joe was thrilled I wanted to meet with him but was surprised to find out why. At first he wasn't listening to me and became defensive. I started to get defensive as well and had to remind myself the goal for our conversation. I calmed down and slowed by speech and softened my voice. Eventually, he understood I cared about his future, him as a person and he started to relax. He shared with me the stresses of his personal life and his need to succeed at work. He didn't realize the impact he was having on his colleagues. He shared his desire to be a leader in the organization and we discussed the behaviors of a leader he wants to emulate. We left the meeting feeling good and headed in the right direction.

SUMMARY

As you can see, dealing with emotions can be challenging but it doesn't have to be impossibly difficult now that you have the EI Blueprint and an understanding of how the abilities work together. This knowledge, along with a lot of practice and constructive feedback, will help you establish trusting relationships and hopefully lead to greater success for yourself, your team and your organization. Part 2 of this Guide are examples of challenges you will undoubtedly face as a leader, along with suggestions on how to apply the EI Blueprint in each situation.

Emotions at work, when used effectively, can propel organizations and their leaders to greatness, or when used ineffectively, can lead organizations and their leaders to stagnation and destruction. Emotions are that important. Emotions are what build relationships and trust. They connect people and are the fabric of what makes life meaningful. They can be channeled to inspire, motivate and innovate. Will you be an emotionally intelligent leader or allow emotions to lead you? Will you role model emotional intelligence, share with others what you have learned and embed it in how you lead so it becomes part of your organizational culture? Dealing with happy people is easy—dealing with people who are experiencing anger or sadness takes great care, a lot of knowledge and finely-honed skill. At times, it may take even higher levels of skill and knowledge when leading a team lacking motivation. Forming relationships and establishing trust in business is the bedrock of leadership. The choice you have is how you interact with emotions at work—emotions exist, emotions matter—whether you perceive them or not. Ignore them or suppress them, they still exist and impact every aspect of leadership.

Ask yourself:

- ✓ Can I accurately Map emotion in myself and others?
- ✓ Do I Match emotions to accomplish the task at hand and connect to others?
- ✓ Do I understand the Meaning of the emotions of others and what motivates, inspires, worries and frustrates them?

✓ Do I effectively Move my emotions and those of others so we can reach our goals?

If you answered yes to these questions, take an additional step: how do you know? Consider whether it is possible you are wrong, and then check your perceptions with others. If the answers are still "yes", terrific, you have a powerful tool you can use in your personal and professional life. If you answered "sometimes"—don't worry. With practice, and more importantly, with corrective feedback, you will improve. It does take time, but if you really care about it, you'll keep practicing and asking for input and observing your behavior and people's reactions.

And if the answer is "no" to the previous questions, don't despair. That you read this guide is a wonderful first step. We don't know if your underlying ability can be improved—perhaps it can. But we do know that you can learn compensatory strategies. Consider spatial intelligence—if it's low, you get lost when heading someplace new for the first time. Can we make you more spatially intelligent? The answer does not matter because we can give you GPS and you will never get lost again (unless, of course, the GPS breaks, just as these strategies may sometimes break down!). Think of the ideas in this book as your GPS for emotions. The goal of this book is to provide you with strategies to improve your leadership performance.

Getting this right—even for those who are skilled—is not easy. For advanced development, there are coaches who specialize in EI who can help you hone EI skills. In the last section, you will find additional information, research and resources for you to continue your EI journey. We wish you all the best!

PART TWO

SOLVING TOUGH LEADERSHIP CHALLENGES WITH EMOTIONAL INTELLIGENCE BLUEPRINTS

WE GET IT, YOU HAVE A LOT GOING ON, AND DON'T HAVE spare time to engage in self-development. The good news about the ability model of EI is there are things you can do now to improve your leadership skills and effectiveness that do not require days, weeks and months of work. This is where your innate intelligence, your analytical ability or IQ, comes into play. In our approach, IQ and EI (we try to avoid using the term "EQ") are related, they are both a type of intelligence, and they can aid one another. Use one kind of smarts to enhance the other. To help you out, we present a series of EI Blueprints to help you grapple with and succeed at the everyday challenges of leadership.

Our Blueprints may not exactly mirror your situation, so this is where your analytical ability comes into play. Analyze your situation, seek out the best matching Blueprint and then adapt it to your specific situation. Even better, use the generic Blueprint process to create and then evaluate your own circumstance—the Blueprint is generic and can be applied very broadly. As you engage in the behaviors suggested by a specific Blueprint, determine how you are feeling

(Map) and whether those feelings are helpful or not (Match). Determine how the situation might unfold (Meaning) and manage (Move) your emotions and those of others in real-time to achieve your goal. Our Blueprints are loosely based on situations we found ourselves in, situations we observed and leadership challenges faced by our clients. We've selected some of the more common issues you will face and organized them into these categories:

- Leading Employees and Teams
- Leading Up and Across
- Common Work Challenges

As you read these Blueprints you might think they seem easy and straightforward. And they are when you simply read them. The key is being able to apply these skills at a high level of expertise, on a consistent basis, in real time, AND under stressful conditions.

By reading through and creating your own Blueprints, you increase the odds that you will enhance your skills and be able to understand the root cause of emotions, use emotions to connect and engage with others, and achieve important goals.

We'd love to hear from *you* with stories of your own challenges and how you addressed them using an *EI Blueprint*[14].

---

14   Send us an email at blueprint@eiskills.com.

EI LEADER BLUEPRINTS—
LEADING EMPLOYEES AND TEAMS

LEADING AN
ANXIOUS TEAM

BACKGROUND When our State Governor declared a state of emergency and issued a stay-at-home order, as the President of a manufacturing business, I knew this could be the end of our company. My first concern is the safety and health of my employees, but quite honestly, I'm more concerned about going out of business. The employees are reeling dealing with homeschooling, uncertainty of the future and concern for their loved ones. I am concerned as well, but I must give them hope of a better tomorrow and I need to do it now to give the employees some peace of mind.

GOAL Calm the fears of the workforce and provide hope for a prosperous future.

EI BLUEPRINT

OUTCOME This was the most difficult meeting of my life. Looking at all of the faces over Zoom and not being able to comfort them was almost more than I could bear, but I had to and I did. During my run before the meeting, I ran through my speech, imagining how they would react. I reminded myself over and over to practice empathy and compassion. The employees could see how much I cared for them on a personal and professional level. I was right – people were sad, angry, worried and depressed. But as I assured them that me and my leadership team was there for them, and they would be getting paid, I could see people relax and some even smiled. I vowed I would stay in constant communication and be as transparent as possible about the future of our company.

STEP	WHAT TO DO
MAP	**What are the emotions of you and others?** I am *worried* about the health of my employees and sustainability of the company. I am *frightened* the pandemic may cripple not only our company, but the world. My employees are *anxious, shocked, depressed, frustrated* and *angry* about their livelihood and future existence.
MATCH	**What emotions are most helpful?** I take a little comfort knowing everyone is feeling stressed about the situation and no one is left unscathed. It is normal to feel how we are feeling. When we are threatened, it is common to feel fear, but fear will not give us the courage to face each day with hope.
MEANING	**What is the cause of these emotions?** I was hired to lead change and if I don't produce a strategic plan, it's over for me. My future is riding on this initiative and I can't do it alone—I need my team. I understand why my team feels the way they do. I'm new; their previous boss didn't care about strategy and I'm pushing them hard. It's no wonder they're avoiding me.
MOVE	**How will you sustain or move these emotions?** All employees have been sent home and frequent, transparent communication is critical from me and my leadership team. I plan on calling an all-hands virtual meeting to assure my employees their jobs are safe. I will ensure I prepare for this meeting as I know it will be difficult. I am predicting some intense unpleasant emotions such as anger, fear and sadness and I must ensure my own emotions are in check. Before the meeting, I will go for a run, which always puts me in a better frame of mind. I will also have my favorite mantra written down in front of me – I have breath, I have balance, I am ok – and look at it throughout the meeting. Most important, I will practice empathy and compassion throughout the meeting. Each employee has their own story and its important I show concern and allow people to share their feelings without shutting them down. I will also announce they will continue to get paid throughout the shutdown, and hopefully give them peace of mind that their jobs will be waiting.

LEADING TEAMS IN STRATEGIC PLANNING AND VISIONING

BACKGROUND I was hired by my company to lead change and inherited a team who, unfortunately, never prioritized strategic planning. I feel it is critical to the success of our company and I need to get my team motivated and engaged in the process. I've tried to discuss the need for planning and visioning and all I get is push-back. We are running out of time and I need to lead the effort or our company may become obsolete.

GOAL Engage the team in strategic planning and visioning and get commitment on moving the company forward in a positive direction.

EI BLUEPRINT

STRATEGIES USED Prepare; Modify Mood; Select Situation; Modulate Tone; Emotional Connection.

OUTCOME Preparing before the meeting was extremely helpful. Visualizing how I wanted the meeting to go actually put me in a better frame of mind. I could tell when I walked in the room that they were waiting for me to dive right into the planning session like a madman. They were quite surprised by my approach and enjoyed the small talk over breakfast before we began. They appreciated my honesty and why I wanted to do strategic planning and that I needed them and wanted them involved in the process. I tried my best not to force my agenda and I was pleased that once I backed off, they engaged. The meeting surpassed my expectations. They left feeling valued, committed and excited about their future and the future of our company.

STEP	WHAT TO DO
MAP	**What are the emotions of you and others?** I am *worried* about the future of the company. I was hired to lead change and I am *frustrated* that I am the only one who sees the urgency. I am worried that if my team doesn't see its importance that we may all be out of a job—starting with me. My team seems a bit *apathetic* and *complacent* about the future and they also seem resistant to me leading the effort.
MATCH	**What emotions are most helpful?** It sounds odd but a bit of anxiety might be useful. Showing worry and urgency might help my team realize the seriousness and importance of planning and visioning. I also don't want to throw a wet blanket on the process, so I also need to be upbeat and positive as we look to the future.
MEANING	**What is the cause of these emotions?** I was hired to lead change and if I don't produce a strategic plan, it's over for me. My future is riding on this initiative and I can't do it alone—I need my team. I understand why my team feels the way they do. I'm new, their previous boss didn't care about strategy and I'm pushing them hard. It's no wonder they're avoiding me.
MOVE	**How will you sustain or move these emotions?** In order to reach the goal I have to manage my emotions. I know that my team senses my urgency, impatience and frustration which is preventing them from engaging with me. Before the meeting I am going to make sure that I relax and envision what a successful meeting will look like. I will enter the room calmly and begin with small talk—heck, I might even bring bagels and coffee. I will then explain why strategic planning is so important and what it can do for our company. And, I'll get them engaged by telling them how they can play a major role in the future of our company. If our company is successful, they will be successful. My hope is that I'll set the stage where people will want to collaborate, get excited about the future and engage as colleagues so that we leave the session feeling positive.

GIVING FEEDBACK TO AN UNDERPERFORMING EMPLOYEE

BACKGROUND When Steve began working for me a year ago, he had a great attitude and was performing at or above my expectations. Lately, I've noticed the quality of his work is slipping and he no longer meets team and individual goals. I've addressed it once before and haven't seen any improvement, so now it's time for a different approach.

GOAL Understand why Steve continues to underperform and have him take action to improve his performance.

EI BLUEPRINT

STRATEGIES USED Physiological (breathing); Emotional Connection; Relationships; Match and Validate.

OUTCOME Steve expected my usual "attack" strategy, sensing at some level, my frustration. When I chose to express support and empathy instead, he was more open and shared he was having problems at home and thought his work was unaffected and no one would notice. I did not pry but offered to help in any way I could. Steve asked for a flexible schedule for the next 4 to 6 weeks, and I agreed to do a trial for 2 weeks to see how it went. He thanked me profusely and apologized that his home life issues had leaked into his workplace performance. Soon after, I saw an improvement in Steve's performance.

STEP	WHAT TO DO
MAP	**What are the emotions of you and others?** I am *frustrated* with Steve because I gave him similar feedback in our last one on one. I am also *annoyed* he hasn't taken my advice for improving his performance. Steve seems to be *confident* in his abilities and seems unaware there is a problem. Steve may make excuses and act *defensive* and perhaps *surprised* when he learns that I still feel he is underperforming.
MATCH	**What emotions are most helpful?** I know my frustration and annoyance aren't helpful for the meeting. Instead, I will approach him with an open mind. I will practice deep listening and empathy trying to understand his point of view. I will stay positive but firm and provide him with candid feedback on his performance.
MEANING	**What is the cause of these emotions?** I think Steve wants to do a good job. I know he wants a promotion. There is a chance that Steve doesn't have the tools or the support that he needs to succeed. He may even be worried about his job and perhaps his confidence is covering how he really feels. There may even be something going on in his personal life impacting his performance.
MOVE	**How will you sustain or move these emotions?** I will manage my emotions during our conversation allowing me to share—calmly—I am frustrated. My calm demeanor may well get his attention. I will make observations and ask him for his view. I will ask open ended questions such as: What do you like about your job? What strengths do you bring to your job? What will help you do your job better? How can I support you to help you reach your goals? If he gets defensive, I will stay calm and try to get him to focus on positive steps he can take to improve his performance.

DELIVERING DISAPPOINTING
NEWS TO A HIGH ACHIEVER

BACKGROUND: Debbie has been on my team for 5 years, her work is above average, she is a great team member and she aspires to be a supervisor. Recently she applied for a supervisory job but wasn't selected. She really thought she had a shot and I am not looking forward to giving her the disappointing, if not devastating news.

GOAL: Inform Debbie she didn't get the promotion and encourage her to stay positive and motivated.

EI BLUEPRINT

STRATEGIES USED Emotional Connection; Match and Validate, Modulate Tone.

OUTCOME I was right—Debbie took the news quite hard. She was clearly disappointed, but she could see how upset I was too and how much I wanted to help her succeed. I reinforced how great she was and encouraged her not to give up. We agreed to meet every other week to talk about how to demonstrate her leadership capabilities. She left the meeting feeling positive and I am confident she will become a supervisor soon.

STEP	WHAT TO DO
MAP	**What are the emotions of you and others?** I feel *sad* Debbie didn't get the promotion she worked so hard for and I feel *anxious* about having to deliver the news. Debbie is a *positive* and *happy* person but that happy mood may lead to intense *disappointment*. I think the news will *devastate* her and she will be *sad, disappointed* and *discouraged*.
MATCH	**What emotions are most helpful?** Debbie is a sensitive person and I want to take her feelings into consideration and be supportive. I will empathize by saying "I can see how you would feel that way". I also don't want her to give up so I will also remind her how great she is using specific examples, offer her suggestions on how to better position herself the next time a supervisory position is available and be available should she need to discuss this more later, when the initial emotions have settled and she is thinking more clearly.
MEANING	**What is the cause of these emotions?** She works hard and this news will not feel like a fair response. It will take Debbie a few days to bounce back from this setback. I will reinforce her strengths and positive qualities, while providing useful feedback she can use next time she applies.
MOVE	**How will you sustain or move these emotions?** I will check in with Debbie more frequently to ensure she is engaged and passionate about her work. I will offer words of encouragement. I will ensure she has projects where she can excel and provide her with leadership opportunities demonstrating her supervisory abilities.

LAYING OFF AN
UNSATISFACTORY EMPLOYEE

BACKGROUND Trent joined my team 5 1/2 months ago and has been a problem ever since. He is not a team player, the quality of his work is atrocious and is coupled with his bad attitude. After many performance feedback sessions, I realize that, unfortunately, Trent isn't a good fit for our company. It's time to let him go before the 6-month probationary period is over and I'm the lucky one giving him the news.

GOAL Inform Trent he is being laid off and the reasons why while staying professional.

EI BLUEPRINT

STRATEGIES USED Prepare; Modify Mood; Intervening Moment; Physiological; Modulate Tone.

OUTCOME Before the meeting, I was really anxious so I did some deep breathing to calm down. I reminded myself this decision was best for the company. Trent did not take the news well, yelling and blaming me for his poor performance. I carefully managed my emotional response by decreasing the volume and cadence of my voice to project calm onto the situation. I remained calm and shared the facts behind the difficult decision. Trent did not want to listen to my feedback and finally got up and stormed out of the room. I was disappointed that he didn't hear my feedback but felt I handled the situation well under the circumstances.

STEP	WHAT TO DO
MAP	**What are the emotions of you and others?** I feel *anxious* about telling Trent he's being let go. I feel *guilty* because he has a young family and he is the sole breadwinner. And, frankly, I am a bit *annoyed* at the time I'm spending on this and my team is *frustrated* by his behavior. Trent knows he is not performing but I don't think he understands the consequences. And if he does, he certainly doesn't show it.
MATCH	**What emotions are most helpful?** This is a serious matter and I need to have a serious tone. I want to provide Trent with facts so he understands why he is being fired. I want to show genuine empathy but have to be careful that his emotions and mine don't distract me from my message. Trent may become defensive and angry so I need to stay calm to deliver the news.
MEANING	**What is the cause of these emotions?** I have given Trent repeated feedback on his perfor-mance. Others have given him feedback which he ignored. The entire team is fed up with his lack of caring and willingness to improve. Trent has been defensive and resistant to feedback and every-thing I have tried has failed.
MOVE	**How will you sustain or move these emo-tions?** I will take time to prepare for the meeting once I'm emotionally ready. During the conversa-tion, I need to remind myself of the goal, breathe and stay focused on what I need to do, however difficult. If Trent gets upset, I will listen, empa-thize and provide him with information he needs to move on. I will stay firm and end the meeting by wishing him well in a polite and professional manner.

RETAINING AN UNDERUTILIZED
TOP-NOTCH EMPLOYEE

BACKGROUND Carolyn has been on my team for 13 months. She is super intelligent with a strong work ethic and high energy. Any project I give her she completes quickly, accurately and willingly. I wish all my employees were as great as Carolyn. Recently, our workload has slowed and I'm running out of projects to give her. She's a real go-getter and if I don't keep her busy, I'm afraid she'll leave my team.

GOAL Discover ways to re-engage Carolyn and retain her talents on the team.

EI BLUEPRINT

STRATEGIES USED Modify Mood; Emotional Connection; Relationships.

OUTCOME Carolyn and I had a great conversation. She really appreciated my honesty and interest in her career goals and strengths. She was definitely disappointed the special projects were drying up. After seeing how much I wanted to help reach her goals, she felt badly that I was worried she was going to leave. I mentored her for several months and she continued to be a superstar. However, six months later she left my team for another division who needed someone to lead special projects. While I was sad to see her go, I was happy to support her and wish her all the best.

STEP	WHAT TO DO
MAP	**What are the emotions of you and others?** I am *worried* I may lose Carolyn. She loves what she does and I am *afraid* that she'll become *disappointed* and *bored* if she's not kept busy. I also feel *guilty* because I have to be equitable to the rest of my team and can't give her all of the new projects in *fear* of losing her. Carolyn has no idea that work is about to slow down and she's really on top of her game feeling *positive, happy* and *engaged.*
MATCH	**What emotions are most helpful?** I can't let my fear of losing Carolyn delay telling her what's happening. She deserves to know. I want to be honest but also give her hope that things will change. I want her to know how much I appreciate her and her work and sustain her positivity and engagement.
MEANING	**What is the cause of these emotions?** Carolyn shared her career goals with me when I hired her. I know she wants to be on a fast track for promotion and believes that taking on special projects is the fastest way to promotion. If she believes that no projects equates to no promotion, she'll go from feeling positive to negative in 10 seconds flat. I rely on Carolyn heavily so losing her would be a blow to my team.
MOVE	**How will you sustain or move these emotions?** I have to overcome my fear of losing Carolyn. I will meet with her to discuss her job and future with our company. Specifically, I want to review her career goals and ask her to share what she likes about her current job. When does she feel excited and challenged? What does she find boring? We will discuss ways to bring her strengths and passion into her routine work. I also need to set her expectations around promotion. Carolyn is a high achiever and she may become impatient with how long it takes. She may also worry that she won't be noticed if she doesn't work on special projects. I will encourage her to stay positive and offer to mentor her to better position herself for a promotion. I feel that honesty and supporting her career goals will help Carolyn find satisfaction in her work even without special projects.

DEALING WITH A DISSATISFIED TEAM

BACKGROUND I have led my team for the past year and think I am a pretty good leader. My team seems happy with my performance and satisfied with their jobs—or so I thought. I received my first formal performance evaluation and the results were quite alarming. The ratings were so low that my boss noticed and wants to know why. The unfortunate part is, I have no idea! Today I have a meeting with my team and as much as I don't want to, I need to raise this issue before it negatively impacts my career.

GOAL Solicit candid feedback from my team to improve employee satisfaction.

EI BLUEPRINT

STRATEGIES USED Modify Mood; Reappraise; Intervening Moment; Select Situation; Emotional Connection; Match and Validate; Physiological.

OUTCOME The group meeting went well but I could tell they were holding back. They could see my concern, but they didn't quite trust my motive. It wasn't until the one-on-ones that I noticed a shift. At first, they were cautious and guarded. I knew I had to carefully manage my emotions so I wouldn't shut them down. I used a list of questions so I didn't lose focus. They could see I was having a difficult time and I really did care about them. They saw I wanted to make changes to improve the work environment and to support them. Some were more receptive than others, but I approached each meeting being vulnerable, curious and humble. Eventually, we got to know each other better and the trust started to build. Now I know what makes each person "tick". Fortunately, investing in relationships worked and my next evaluation showed remarkable improvement—making me, and my boss, very happy.

STEP	WHAT TO DO
MAP	**What are the emotions of you and others?** I thought my team liked me so I feel **surprised, hurt** and honestly, **angry.** I give this team everything I have and feel **betrayed**—this is the thanks I get. They really let me down. The team seems **content**, but the survey results show deep **dissatisfaction.**
MATCH	**What emotions are most helpful?** I am in a bad place emotionally. I cannot walk into the conference room angry or hurt because they will shut down on me immediately. I need to create a safe environment where they open up to me. Instead of being upset, I will be curious. I will bring up my feedback results and share my concerns. I will tell them I take their job satisfaction seriously and my job is to create a pleasant and supportive work environment. My hope is that they will see my concern and I'll get the feedback I need to make positive changes.
MEANING	**What is the cause of these emotions?** I understand why I am disappointed in my team's feedback. I thought I was doing all the right things, and apparently, I am not. In reflecting on why my team feels dissatisfied, I hate to admit it, but I have no idea. I haven't spent time getting to know what makes them satisfied and in return, they chose my performance feedback to let me know exactly how they feel.
MOVE	**How will you sustain or move these emotions?** To get them to open up, I can't be defensive or angry about the results. Instead, I will go into the meeting feeling calm and pleasant. I will show concern about the feedback and REALLY listen to them to make sure I understand the issues. I will also schedule one-one-one meetings to get to know them better. We'll talk about their career goals, what they enjoy about work, what bores or frustrates them, what they like to do for fun and what's important to them. I will also do the same and share things. about me they may not know. I hope connecting with them on a more personal level will help build trust and hopefully improve their satisfaction going forward.

BACKGROUND I have led my team for the past 5 years and our meetings have become unfocused, disorganized and downright boring. It's getting to the point where I don't even want to have them and I think my team feels the same. Meetings have become a waste of time and if something doesn't change soon, people will permanently check out and disengage—and not just in meetings.

GOAL Conduct weekly meetings that connect and re-engage our team.

EI BLUEPRINT

STRATEGIES USED Modify Mood; Self-talk; Select Situation; Change Situation; Emotional Connection; Reappraise; Intervening Moment.

OUTCOME The meeting didn't go exactly as planned. While I prepared for the meeting by taking a walk and psyching myself up beforehand, I didn't prepare for their possible reactions. I knew they might be resistant to my request, but I was shocked with what happened. I started the meeting by sharing how I didn't like our meetings and they immediately attacked me. They said it was my fault the meetings were so awful and got really angry with me. I realize now that I should have started with taking responsibility and my goal for our meetings. We took a quick break to recover from my shock and started over from where I should have begun—acknowledging my part and their feelings. Eventually, we discussed the pressures of the job and the goal for our meetings. Once we had the goal in mind, we brainstormed ways to make them more engaging and meaningful. It took us a while to engage, but we left committed to our meetings and each other.

STEP	WHAT TO DO
MAP	**What are the emotions of you and others?** Even though I lead the meetings, I must admit I am feeling *bored, unmotivated* and *disinterested* during our meetings. I know my team is *annoyed* and *irritated* at wasting their time meeting when they could do something more productive.
MATCH	**What emotions are most helpful?** Unfortunately, we dread meetings instead of looking forward to them. I want our meetings to be engaging, positive and supportive.
MEANING	**What is the cause of these emotions?** I'll be honest. We are burned out. We have so much on our plate. Instead of attending wasteful meetings we want to make sales calls and visit clients. The only results of our meetings are irritation, disappointment and anxiety.
MOVE	**How will you sustain or move these emotions?** Meetings are important because they offer an opportunity to share, get updates that impact our work and collaborate on important projects. I need to shift us from disengagement to engagement. First, I need to get in the right state of mind, so I go into the meeting feeling upbeat and energized. I will take responsibility for the tone of our recent meetings and ask for their help in making them what they used to be—a place where we felt engaged, supported and productive. They may meet me with resistance because they are so busy, but I'll keep telling myself to smile, show empathy and be persistent.

LEADING
VIRTUAL TEAMS

BACKGROUND I lead a team of 12 professionals located in four geographic locations. Each employee has his/her own area of responsibility and enjoys a high level of autonomy. The challenge is we only see each other by video once a week for an hour. I have noticed some people don't seem engaged and there is no sense of team. I am at a loss how to re-engage the team and how to find our esprit de corp.

GOAL Build trust and camaraderie among a virtual team.

EI BLUEPRINT

STRATEGIES USED Modify Mood; Modulate Tone; Emotional Connection.

OUTCOME I scheduled my one-on-one meetings and made a big error. I didn't tell them why I wanted to meet with them. Some people were alarmed that I wanted to meet with them. Not a good way to begin a meeting! Once they understood the reason for my meeting they were relieved and slowly became engaged. The virtual meetings were more difficult. I tried my best to match the emotion of the other person so I didn't overwhelm them. I smiled a lot and my voice conveyed positivity and interest. I believe the meetings were successful and I noticed my team started engaging more in meetings once I changed the format. We are looking forward to coming together in person in a few months and I am confident it will strengthen my team even more.

STEP	WHAT TO DO
MAP	**What are the emotions of you and others?** I am *worried* that my team is splintered and feeling *isolated*. They don't seem to share and perhaps they don't trust each other. I have seen some *frustration* and even *apathy* from my team during our meetings.
MATCH	**What emotions are most helpful?** I want my team to feel happy to be together. I want them to be positive and look forward to seeing each other. I want them to feel safe to share challenges and work together collegially and collaboratively.
MEANING	**What is the cause of these emotions?** Being on a virtual team is tough. We only see each other for an hour a week and some use video and some do not. Some share a lot and some do not. Because each person is so specialized there isn't an understanding of what others do and therefore, no way to support others if they are challenged. People are polite but superficial. I understand why they are disengaged.
MOVE	*How will you sustain or move these emotions?* We haven't had an in-person meeting with the entire team for over a year. Since that time 5 people have joined my team. If I can bring them together, I think it will help build relationships and trust. However, I haven't really gotten to know my team, or they me. First, I am going to have a one-on-one to build relationships. I need to know what makes them happy, frustrated, bored and proud. I will meet with them one-on-one on a weekly basis. I will change our weekly meeting agenda. Instead of asking people what they are working on, they will be expected to share a work success, something they are excited about and a challenge the team can help resolve. If they don't have anything to share, I will ask them to discuss what they are working on so others can better understand their area of responsibility. We will also spend a few minutes checking in about what else is happening with each person – starting with me to model the behavior to help create an atmosphere of trust and camaraderie.

BACKGROUND I always make hiring decisions with input from my team but as division head, I make the final decision. We have a key job opening and Jose and Veronica were the final candidates we interviewed. The team is very excited about Jose but do not hold Veronica in high regard. Jose is dynamic, witty and engaging and seemed more like a friend than a job candidate. Veronica was more low-key and introspective, but her skills are superb. She displayed great judgment, gave thoughtful responses and had a refreshing openness about herself. I definitely want to hire Veronica and know doing so will cause disharmony in the ranks.

GOAL Help my team understand and support my hiring decision.

EI BLUEPRINT

STRATEGIES USED Prepare; Reappraise; Select Situation; Intervening Moment; Match and Validate.

OUTCOME I started the meeting with a flip chart and markers and we began listing strengths of each candidate. It was going well until they could sense how much I wanted to hire Veronica. They became defensive and angry that I was doing a sell job and felt strong armed into agreeing with me. Instead of being on the same page, we became more divided. After a 15-minute break we reconvened and I told them I did value their opinion and could see why Jose would be great for the team. Once I relaxed and stayed open to their feedback they relaxed as well. We were then able to have a meaningful conversation focusing on who was best for our organization. They felt heard and valued and despite the rough start, we all decided that Veronica was the better choice for our organization.

STEP	WHAT TO DO
MAP	**What are the emotions of you and others?** I am *excited* about Veronica. The team is ***pleased*** and ***excited*** about Jose and neutral towards Veronica. They also feel ***assured*** that I will hire Jose. I am ***worried*** they will feel ***angry*** and ***unappreciated*** when I hire Veronica instead.
MATCH	**What emotions are most helpful?** Their high level of excitement is not helpful. They are being overly positive imagining how Jose will fit right in and not looking at him objectively. Veronica's lack of charm focused them on her lackluster job interview, and they don't think she's a good fit for the team. However, my restrained approach allowed me to see strengths and weaknesses of both candidates and helped me make the right choice.
MEANING	**What is the cause of these emotions?** My team is terrific and for the most part are positive, upbeat and optimistic. They connected with Jose, who shares their temperament. I understand their enthusiasm and know they will be disappointed with my decision. I will do my best to help them understand why I chose Veronica.
MOVE	**How will you sustain or move these emotions?** Before giving the news, I will take a few minutes to prepare because this meeting won't be easy. I'm anticipating surprise, frustration, annoyance and resistance which means they will totally shut me down and not hear why I selected Veronica. I will begin by asking them to list the strengths of both candidates. I will ask them what they liked about each candidate. I will focus them on the role this person will have and how each strength aligns to the job. I will help move their emotion by keeping them focused and challenge them to be objective. My hope is that in the end they see Veronica as a stronger candidate. However, this approach may backfire if they still see Jose as a stronger candidate.

EI LEADER BLUEPRINTS—
LEADING UP AND ACROSS

BACKGROUND Jennifer has been my boss for almost 3 years. When she hired me she was really excited about what I could bring to the team and put me in charge of a new division. Jenn and I used to be quite close, almost friends, but things changed. Now, she frequently criticizes me and my team and yells in meetings. I don't know how much longer I can endure her volatile behavior.

GOAL Understand my boss' behavior and improve the work environment.

EI BLUEPRINT

STRATEGIES USED Prepare; Modify Mood; Reappraise; Self-talk; Physiological Techniques; Intervening Moment; Select Situation; Change Situation; Match and Validate; Modulate Tone; Emotional Connection.

OUTCOME This was one of the most difficult conversations I've had. I spent a lot of time preparing for the meeting. I envisioned what might happen, how I would state the issue and what I would do if she reacted negatively. I also meditated and told myself that everything would be ok - I was doing the right thing. Knowing she hates when I show emotion, I kept the conversation very factual keeping my emotions neutral. She started raising her voice and I practiced deep breathing, reminding myself of my goal. Calmly I waited and asked politely her expectations of me and my team. I asked if there was anything we were doing to upset her. Eventually, her anger subsided, and she started to cry. She shared her illness was sapping her energy and she didn't feel she could lead at the same level as before. She even shared the medicine she takes results in mood swings. She apologized profusely and felt badly for the havoc she created. After our meeting, she was courageous in sharing her condition with my team. I am grateful that she shared what was happening and even though we aren't as close as we were, we have a much better relationship than before.

STEP	WHAT TO DO
MAP	**What are the emotions of you and others?** I am *worried* that my boss has lost confidence in me. I get *nervous* every time I talk with her, *afraid* that I may do or say something wrong. I am also *angry* she is treating my team badly and they're *afraid* of her. It's obvious that Jenn is feeling *angry*, *hostile* and *volatile*.
MATCH	**What emotions are most helpful?** My emotions are shutting down my ability to effectively communicate, produce and create. Her anger is infecting everyone around the office and the team is on pins and needles. We should be collaborating, creating new products and enjoying the team spirit we used to enjoy not long ago.
MEANING	**What is the cause of these emotions?** Jenn has been under enormous stress lately. Her boss is coming down on her questioning her actions. Perhaps she is worried that she may lose her job. I also know she was in the hospital recently. Her illness may be contributing to her emotional state. It's also possible I may not be meeting her needs and she wants something else from me.
MOVE	**How will you sustain or move these emotions?** Even though I dread it, I must have a meeting with Jenn. I need to be cautious because she is already angry. Therefore, I will take time to prepare for our meeting. Instead of being on edge, I will show up calm and ready to listen. I also need to make sure my boss is in a good place so I'll schedule the meeting when she is feeling calm. I will monitor my tone of voice and body language because if she senses anger or sadness, she will shut me down. I will prepare a few good questions and statements to help me stay focused on the goal for our meeting. I want to leave the meeting knowing what she expects from me and my team going forward.

DEALING WITH A
DISENGAGED BOSS

BACKGROUND I am a high achiever and want to add value to my organization. My boss, Will, hired me because he knew I had potential and I was excited because he seemed like a great mentor. I really enjoy picking his brain, running projects by him and sharing my interests. After a few months, I noticed he kept cancelling our one-on-one meetings and rarely called, emailed or visited my office. When I stop by his office to check in, he seems distracted. We haven't had a meaningful conversation in weeks, and I can't help wondering if I did something to make him avoid me.

GOAL Reconnect with my boss and get the support I need to be successful in my career.

EI BLUEPRINT

STRATEGIES USED Modify Mood; Reappraise; Self-talk; Emotional Connection; Match and Validate.

OUTCOME Will and I had a great meeting; I mentioned how we haven't been meeting as much as we used to and I really miss his guidance. He was so surprised. He thought because I was doing so well, I didn't need him anymore. He didn't want to micromanage, so he made it a point to distance himself. Once I told him how much I valued our meetings, he was pleased. We agreed to meet once a month for mentoring meetings rather than working meetings. Our meetings have been great and I'm so glad I brought it up to Will rather than ignore my feelings.

STEP	WHAT TO DO
MAP	**What are the emotions of you and others**? I feel *abandoned* by my boss and this makes me feel *disappointed* and a little *anxious*. I'm also very *confused* about what's going on. Will seems *apathetic*, *disengaged* and even *disinterested* at times.
MATCH	**What emotions are most helpful**? Over the last month, I have lost enthusiasm for work and my productivity is suffering. I was feeling positive, but now I've turned negative and see the negative impact I'm having on others. I need to get my positivity back!
MEANING	**What is the cause of these emotions?** I am a people person and like having a close relationship with my boss. It means the world to me to feel supported and cared for and not feeling connected to Will is causing me to feel depressed. Will may be disengaged because of something I did but perhaps there is something else going on that doesn't even relate to me.
MOVE	**How will you sustain or move these emotions?** I want to be positive during our meeting and open to his feedback. I want him to know how much I value his guidance. If his behavior is because of me, I will ask what he needs from me. And if it isn't related to me, I'll show concern and empathy and ask how I can help support him.

BACKGROUND I have worked for Jeff as his Chief Financial Officer for the past ten years. Jeff is a great guy and as our Executive Director, he really cares about the organization. Being a non-profit, we rely on our donors more and more as the economy and government funding tightens. Last night Jeff came to me after hours asking how we record one of our liabilities. He asked if I could re-categorize the liability to improve the bottom line. I explained we couldn't because it violated accounting guidelines. He kept persisting and finally after a heated exchange told me—just do it. Unfortunately, it isn't that easy and I now have to deal with what could be a career-ending decision.

GOAL Understand my boss' behavior and ethically resolve the situation.

EI BLUEPRINT

STRATEGIES USED Modify Mood; Reappraise; Physiological; Emotional Connection; Relationships; Match and Validate; Modulate Tone.

OUTCOME This was a tough meeting. I am Jeff's friend and I knew he would be disappointed in his behavior. I started from a place of care and concern and at first, he denied anything was wrong. I mentioned the declining revenue and support from our donors and asked if he was concerned. He slowly started to open up how his biggest fear was not being able to serve those in need. He started to choke up with emotion. I let him share and get it all out. I told him what he was asking me to do wasn't going to fix our problem. I told him together, and with the team's and board's help, we could figure it out. He was relieved to realize he wasn't alone. He was embarrassed and disappointed in what he asked me to do. He asked if I would forgive him and help him move forward in finding ethical, collaborative solutions. I did and fortunately we were able to turn the organization around before it was too late.

STEP	WHAT TO DO
MAP	**What are the emotions of you and others?** I am *shocked* that Jeff would even ask me to do something remotely unethical. I am *anxious* I could get in trouble if I do what he wants. I am *worried* I may lose my CPA license, my job, my integrity and my self-respect. I am also *angry* Jeff is putting me in this position. I thought we were friends. I am sure Jeff is *worried* about the future of our organization—one he helped begin. He may even feel *guilty* for asking me to do something unethical.
MATCH	**What emotions are most helpful?** I know my tremendous anxiety is clouding my ability to think and be productive. This is not where I want or need to be—especially with our future at stake. We are presenting our financial statements in a week and all I can think of is the mess we're in. I need to be a little more relaxed.
MEANING	**What is the cause of these emotions?** Jeff has been the Director of our organization for over a decade. He loves this organization and would do anything to ensure that we offer services to the underserved. I know he is very concerned our donations have fallen off and our investments haven't produced as hoped. Jeff is a good guy and I know he knows what he is asking me to do is wrong.
MOVE	**How will you sustain or move these emotions?** I will schedule our meeting at the end of the day when Jeff is more relaxed. During our meeting, I will connect with him on the great work we are doing and thank him for everything he has done for the staff and clients. I want him to know how much people care about him and appreciate his servant leadership. I will tell him I want him to be the Director for many years to come but am concerned about what he asked me to do. I will ask him to explain why he wants to have me do something that could risk our future. I don't want him to be defensive or angry so I will stay calm and listen. I will tell him he is not alone and has the support of his staff, the board and our clients. Together, we will come up with a solution, but it must be above board. My hope is he realizes the severity of the situation and will move forward in finding a collaborative, ethical solution.

BACKGROUND I have worked with Ann for five years. She works in our home office and I work in the field. We frequently work together on special projects and lately Ann has been acting like she is working alone on our projects. I have come up with some great ideas to move our organization forward but during meetings with our boss, Ann takes most of the credit and won't let me get a word in edgewise. I am not sure why she is taking the credit and shooting my ideas down but it's time to find out before I lose my temper.

GOAL Work more effectively with my colleague.

EI BLUEPRINT

STRATEGIES USED Prepare; Modify Mood; Self-talk; Physiological; Emotional Connection; Relationships.

OUTCOME I met with Ann shortly after a meeting with our boss where she took credit and didn't let my voice be heard. I did a lot of preparation getting ready for our meeting and began it by sharing my feelings. Ann wasn't surprised by how I felt because she could see my emotions on my face during our meetings. I didn't realize that my displeasure had leaked and if she could see it, I am sure my boss could as well. This was really good feedback for me to hear. I asked her why she took credit for my work and shut me down. I could tell she felt awful when she started to cry. Reluctantly, she acknowledged that she was worried I would get promoted before her. However, she didn't realize she was making herself look good at my expense. It felt good to tell her how I was feeling, and I was relieved that it was unintentional. We vowed that going forward, we would support each other rather than tear each other down. It was an emotional meeting but it worked. As a team we excelled, projects were on target, our boss was happy and we were both promoted the next year.

STEP	WHAT TO DO
MAP	**What are the emotions of you and others?** I am *angry* that my colleague is taking the credit for my work. I am *disappointed* because I thought we were friends. And I'm *worried* and *anxious* my boss won't think I'm pulling my weight. I *dread* working with Ann and am *disengaging* from our joint projects. I don't share my ideas with her anymore and am getting really *discouraged*.
MATCH	**What emotions would be most helpful?** This can't go on much longer because my behavior is having a negative impact on my morale and productivity. I can't avoid Ann forever and need to be proactive in a solution. I want and need to be more positive, engaged and collaborative with Ann.
MEANING	**What is the cause of these emotions?** It's no wonder I feel the way I do because recognition is important to me. I have no issues working on a team and sharing credit. I've always been a team player. I know that Ann is trying to get promoted and perhaps this is why she takes more credit. I also know that Ann is not a "big idea" person and her strength is more in the details. She could be trying to portray herself differently and doing it by stealing my ideas.
MOVE	**How will you sustain or move these emotions?** Ann and I need to resolve our situation soon. If we don't, it will negatively impact our future success. We won't get our projects done and our boss will think we are incompetent. Ann and I share the same goals—bring innovative products to our clients and be professionally successful. Before our meeting, I am going to take time to mentally prepare. I am going to practice deep breathing to make sure I am calm. I am going to try to anticipate her reaction and write down a few thoughts and questions I can ask her to ensure we have a productive meeting. During the meeting, I will move my emotions and ensure I stay level headed. I will let her know I think we make a great team and appreciate what she brings to our team. I will ask her about her career goals and will share mine. I will ask her how she feels about working on projects with me and how we can work better together. I will also ask her how we can brief our boss to ensure both our voices are heard. I will end the meeting on a positive note and let her know I am looking forward to working with her on future projects. I'm really hoping our conversation will improve our relationship going forward.

WORKING WITH A VOLUNTEER
BOARD OF DIRECTORS

BACKGROUND I became CEO of a non-profit a little over a year ago and am employed at the discretion of a volunteer board of directors. The Board Chair has held this position for 20 years and most of the board members have been on our board for 20+ years. I am noticing signs of dysfunction at our board meetings and don't feel they have the organization's best interest when making decisions. I am new to my job and don't want to upset the board, but if they don't get more engaged soon, our non-profit could be headed for trouble.

GOAL Engage the board to operate at their full capability and capacity.

EI BLUEPRINT

STRATEGIES USED Modify Mood; Reappraise; Emotional Connection.

OUTCOME I met with the Board Chair after our last board meeting. It was a typical meeting with bickering and lack of focus so it was a perfect time to discuss what was happening. At first he was quite defensive and denied there were issues. However, as I discussed what I was seeing, he admitted he saw it too, but didn't know what to do about it and was relieved I wanted to help. We talked about holding a 2-day off-site strategic visioning retreat with the Board and my leadership team around the future of the organization. We agreed to have it professionally facilitated with a blend of team building and future planning. That way everyone can get to know each other on a personal level as well as have a common goal of focusing on our organization's mission and possibilities for the future. We both left the meeting feeling hopeful that the retreat would refocus, re-engage and re-energize all of us.

STEP	WHAT TO DO
MAP	**What are the emotions of you and others?** I am *shocked* by the lack of respect between board members. I am *concerned* that personalities are getting in the way of doing what is best for the people we serve. My leadership is also *confused* as to what the board expects and we are *worried* about the direction, or lack of direction, about our future. The board acts *hostile* during our monthly meetings towards each other and my leadership team. They seem *displeased* with our strategic vision yet they won't share why.
MATCH	**What emotions would be most helpful?** Our current emotional state is hindering our ability to collaborate and communicate effectively. We need to feel safe to engage in difficult topics about the future of our organization. We need to be collegial and collaborative and suspend judgement while staying open to differing options and possibilities.
MEANING	**What is the cause of these emotions?** I am new and perhaps they are comparing me to the previous CEO. The prior CEO made all of the decisions and told the board what to do, not the other way around. We also have some new members on the board who want to lead change and engage more in discussions. I am sensing the seasoned board members feel threatened and challenged by this new approach. They have voiced their concerns about lack of cohesiveness and collaboration and it is making the other board members uncomfortable and defensive.
MOVE	**How will you sustain or move these emotions?** We are grateful to have dedicated volunteers on our board who have a wealth of experience. They truly do care about our clients and want to do the right thing. I feel that we have been so concerned about the status quo or defending past actions that we've forgotten to envision the future we want to create for our employees and clients. If we can rally together around our mission and future, I feel that the other negative emotions will subside and be replaced with excitement and commitment. I will reach out to the Board Chair to talk about what I am seeing and propose several meetings around strategic visioning and planning.

WORKING WITH AN
UNMOTIVATED COLLEAGUE

BACKGROUND Our team works hard, or at least most of us do. There's one person on our team you just can't count on. We run around like mad men while our colleague Jillian just coasts and it's really starting to negatively impact me. Nothing is ever urgent to her, and she is the most unmotivated person I've ever worked with. We try to be all for one and one for all, but no one wants to work with her anymore. Projects she leads languish and she takes no responsibility for her actions. We've just about given up and it seems like she just doesn't notice, or just doesn't care.

GOAL Hold our colleague accountable for her work and renew our sense of team.

EI BLUEPRINT

STRATEGIES USED Physiological; Self talk; Intervening Moment; Reappraise.

OUTCOME Jillian and I had a project that was 2 weeks behind and I had to speak with her to get it back on track. I knew I was an emotional wreck feeling blame, frustration, disgust and anger towards Jillian and none of those emotions were going to be useful during my meeting. Before the meeting I listened to relaxing music, went for a walk outdoors and quieted my mind. I went into the meeting feeling positive about the great work we had done with a goal of how to get it over the finish line. I anticipated Jillian's reaction that she may not see the urgency or importance of the project. I was very unemotional and stuck to the facts on the status of the project and asked her what we needed to do to finish. She didn't think she had to do anything, so I asked her what I needed to do to finish. She came up with a list and instead of feeling resentful, I thanked her and headed for the door. The project was completed a week later. I know that Jillian will never change unless our boss intervenes. However, I can focus on what I can control—my emotions toward Jillian. Some days it takes more work than others, but I'm trying!

STEP	WHAT TO DO
MAP	**What are the emotions of you and others?** Mine are clear – I am really *annoyed*, a bit *jealous* and *resentful* that our boss lets her slack off and *worried* that her lack of work will negatively impact the work I do. My colleagues are *disgusted* with her. Her emotions are tougher to figure out because she never seems to *worry*, never is *anxious* and everything is always "really good".
MATCH	**What emotions are most helpful?** I realize the negative emotions I harbor towards Jillian are throwing me off my game. I am not doing my best work because I am focusing on what Jillian isn't doing instead of my own work. I need to stay engaged in my work and not get sucked into the drama.
MEANING	**What is the cause of these emotions?** I am up for promotion next year and I need to bring my A game everyday. I work long hours and deliver my projects on time and on budget. Unfortunately, I rely on Jillian for my success and if she doesn't deliver, I don't deliver. Her lack of drive and accountability go totally against my values and it's impacting my work and could impact my career. Jillian doesn't seem to be worried because our boss doesn't hold her accountable for her delays. Why should she be concerned if our boss isn't?
MOVE	**How will you sustain or move these emotions?** In order to stay focused on my job it means I can't focus on Jillian. When I see her behaving contrary to my values, and it doesn't impact me, I will practice letting go. I will create a mantra like—"let it go", "stay focused", or "stay positive". However, there are several projects that I need her help with. I need to figure out what is important to Jillian and how to work better with her. She seems like she doesn't care, but what if she did? I will continue to meet with her on our joint projects and stay focused on the task at hand. I know what I need from her and she is the type of person if you ask her for something, she will give it to you. Instead of feeling resentful I will be grateful to get what I need by asking. I have to keep my emotions more neutral and get really clear about how to get what I need from Jillian going forward.

WORKING WITH
UNSUPPORTIVE COLLEAGUES

BACKGROUND I have worked for our company for 7 years. I was recently promoted to Senior Vice President for my leadership skills and my technical expertise. I oversee a team responsible for 50% of our company's profits. The CEO likes me, but for some reason, my colleagues do not. I am trying not to take it personally but I notice they never ask my opinion, never include me in conversations and treat me like I don't even exist. I want to be part of the team but no matter what I do, I can't break into their circle.

GOAL Feel like a valued, integral part of the executive team.

EI BLUEPRINT

STRATEGIES USED Prepare; Physiological; Self-talk; Modify the Mood; Select Situation.

OUTCOME Our next meeting was a disaster! I prepared and was ready to show my personal side and they just ignored me even more. I didn't cry but they could clearly see I was breaking down. After I gathered myself, I told them I thought they were ignoring me, and I felt alone. Thankfully, they showed me great empathy and explained the reason they hadn't warmed to me: I asked too many questions and didn't listen. They felt I was discounting their experience and not open to their feedback. I could see how my naive questions and suggestions were coming across as rejecting their contributions. They told me they were happy to have me on the team and welcomed my ideas and enthusiasm. But, I didn't take time to learn the lay of the land and to listen instead of speaking. It was an invaluable lesson. I began listening more and eventually I became an integral part of the team.

STEP	WHAT TO DO
MAP	**What are the emotions of you and others?** I feel *rejected, isolated* and *alienated*. Also, a bit *confused* as to why my colleagues, who seem like nice people, are avoiding me. As for my colleagues, I am not sure how they feel. They are very *pleasant* with each other but are *disinterested* and *annoye*d towards me.
MATCH	**What emotions are most helpful?** My isolation veers towards sadness at times, especially in meetings when they ignore me. I am sure they can see the pain on my face. I don't want them to think I'm an emotional wreck or a needy person so I do my best to hide how I feel. No wonder I hate attending meetings with them. I want them to see me as interesting, fun and engaging so they'll want to include me in conversations and ask my opinions.
MEANING	**What is the cause of these emotions?** No matter how hard I try, I feel rejected at every turn. The more I'm rejected, the sadder and more depressed I become. I am not sure why my colleagues are ignoring me. Perhaps they resent my promotion or how much revenue I bring to the company. Could they even feel a bit jealous? I am the youngest member of the executive team so maybe they don't take me seriously.
MOVE	**How will you sustain or move these emotions?** I cannot continue to feel like a loner with my colleagues because I know I am a nice person and a great leader. Before our meetings I will remind myself why I was promoted and look for opportunities to add value in the meetings instead of sitting back feeling sorry for myself. I will even show the personal side of me, showing vulnerability and letting them see the real me. Once they get to know me and see my value to the company, I know I won't be on the outside much longer.

EI LEADER BLUEPRINTS—
COMMON LEADERSHIP CHALLENGES

DEALING WITH AN
UNHAPPY CLIENT

BACKGROUND For the past 10 years, we have enjoyed a very lucrative and collaborate partnership with a client instrumental to our company's success. Recently, I've noticed something has changed. In meetings the client isn't as collegial, and we haven't done any new business with them for close to a year. As Senior VP of Sales, I am concerned there may be a problem and asked the client to meet with us to discuss the situation.

GOAL Connect with the client to understand their needs and how to better support them.

EI BLUEPRINT

STRATEGIES USED Modify Mood; Self-talk; Physiological Techniques; Match and Validate; Emotional Connection.

OUTCOME I set up the meeting the following week and went to their office. I was upfront about how I noticed a change in our relationship and wanted to confirm my observations. They were surprised I noticed, and appreciative for my concern. Reluctantly, they shared they have been going through internal reorganizations leaving them uncertain of their future. I felt badly for them but relieved it wasn't our fault. I showed care and concern and offered any support to help. They were grateful I took time to come see them. Unfortunately, their reorganization did lead to less business, but the business we do have is productive and our relationship is even stronger than before.

STEP	WHAT TO DO
MAP	**What are the emotions of you and others?** I am **worried** our client may end our relationship and take their business elsewhere. If this happens, I may be viewed as an ineffective leader, be removed from my position and lose the respect of my staff, colleagues and boss. The relationship with the client feels **strained**. In our last meeting I noticed the client seemed very **anxious, impatient, irritated** and even a little **annoyed**.
MATCH	**What emotions are most helpful?** I am allowing my worry to overwhelm me and I'm avoiding them. I need to set up a meeting to really hear what they have to say and must be open to their feedback, no matter how awful it may be. I want them to know how much I appreciate their business and I will show my support.
MEANING	**What is the cause of these emotions?** I know why I am worried about meeting them, but have no idea why they seem upset with us. I realize I haven't had a recent conversation on what is important to them and whether we are meeting their needs. In my next meeting, I will focus on their goals and how I can support them in reaching them. I need to understand where they are now, where they want to be, and how I can help them get there.
MOVE	**How will you sustain or move these emotions?** My worrying about losing the client has prevented me from soliciting their feedback. I need to work on moving my own emotion around this uncomfortable situation. I will practice deep listening and make sure I understand their needs. I will be positive and reflect on the previous successes and work hard to re-establish the relationship we once had.

PRESENTING TO A
SKEPTICAL AUDIENCE

BACKGROUND As the head of Human Resources, I report to the CEO and work closely with the other Senior Vice Presidents. We are experiencing high turnover, grievances for unfair labor practices, low morale, poor customer service and decreased productivity. I have been tasked with coming up with a plan to turn things around and asked to present my recommendations at our next executive meeting.

GOAL Present options that will engage productive discussions and outcomes.

EI BLUEPRINT

STRATEGIES USED Prepare; Modify Mood; Self-talk; Physiological Techniques; Match and Validate; Emotional Connection.

OUTCOME I was right—it was the most difficult presentation I've ever made. I did everything I said I would do to prepare for the meeting. I had the meeting in the morning when I knew we would be at our best and ready to engage. I spent 30 minutes envisioning the meeting and practiced deep breathing as I walked around the building. I started my presentation with a serious tone so they knew I understood the importance of the meeting. I watched for signs of negative emotion and it did happen. Instead of ignoring their emotions, I stayed open and allowed them to share their thoughts and really listened to their concerns. They could see how much I cared about the issues we faced and were pleased that I had several ideas for improving the situation. The more I listened, the more people engaged in honest dialogue. I was relieved that they took responsibility for the situation and didn't leave me holding the bag. We left the meeting with ideas of the work that needed to be done to turn things around. Even though we have an incredibly hard road ahead of us, we are more committed to each other and our company. I am so glad I took the time to prepare myself emotionally and was able to successfully move my colleagues' emotions to reach our goal.

STEP	WHAT TO DO
MAP	**What are the emotions of you and others?** I have never been so *nervous* in my entire career. I feel my job is riding on this presentation and I am beyond *worried.* The CEO and my colleagues are *agitated* we haven't figured out and fixed the problem. I *fear* they are *blaming* me.
MATCH	**What emotions are most helpful?** Feeling nervous isn't a bad thing. I should be worried and a little anxious to help me focus on the topic and examine all options carefully. However, I need to make sure I manage my fear and anxiousness so I don't shut down or sound unsure of my recommendations. I want my colleagues to be receptive to what I have to say.
MEANING	**What is the cause of these emotions?** I am on the hot seat because hiring, employee satisfaction, employment issues all fall under my purview. I can't control what other supervisors are doing to cause these issues but I am expected to fix it. My colleagues are frustrated that the problem hasn't gone away and they have other things they rather be doing. They are also concerned that our customers may leave and our employees will quit.
MOVE	**How will you sustain or move these emotions?** I am going to be really nervous and I will take time, a lot of time, to prepare for this presentation. I will get in the right frame of mind by meditating, listening to relaxing music and going for a walk. I will do emotional forecasting about what might happen in the meeting. How might people react to my proposal? I want to make sure that they are open to my suggestions so I will have to carefully monitor their emotions during the meeting. I will practice what I will say, how I will say it, my tone of voice, my body language and will stay positive during my presentation. During the meeting I will focus on our common goal—to improve employee and customer satisfaction and share my ideas for making improvements. But I don't want them to feel that I have it figured out. I want to offer possibilities and engage them in meaningful discussions so we leave with a common goal and commitment of what we will do going forward.

RESPONDING TO AN
ANGRY EMAIL

BACKGROUND: John and I have worked on the same leadership team for the past year. We get along rather well and frequently work together on high-profile initiatives. Our current project is almost complete with the final report due to our CEO tomorrow. Today, out of the blue, I received a scathing email from John accusing me of sabotaging the project and not pulling my weight. He ended the e-mail indicating I didn't care about the project and expressed his disappointment in my behavior. Needless to say, I sat looking at the e-mail for a very long time.

GOAL Respond to the e-mail professionally and resolve the issue immediately.

EI BLUEPRINT

STRATEGIES USED Modify Mood; Reappraise; Self-talk; Physiological; Select Situation; Emotional Connection; Modulate Tone.

OUTCOME I went to John's office and what a mistake! While I had good intentions, I just showed up outside his door—dumb! He was already upset with me and seeing me knocking at his door made him even angrier and defensive. In hindsight, I should have emailed him asking him when he was available to meet. He did invite me in, and I was able to share what I wanted but it was a bumpy start. Thankfully, I brought my notes on where the project was and what I had done, and he was relieved. He also admitted perhaps he overreacted because he gets super short with people when he is stressed out. It ended up being a great conversation and we agreed how to communicate more effectively in the future—especially under stress!

STEP	WHAT TO DO
MAP	**What are the emotions of you and others?** I am *surprised* by this e-mail and *angry* that he accused me of not doing my part. I'm also *hurt* because I've worked my butt off to get this project done. Obviously, by his email, John is *ticked off* and *angry*—and *disappointed* that I let him down.
MATCH	**What emotions are most helpful?** How we feel right now is definitely not helpful to either one of us. We need to be collegial, collaborative and motivated if we're going to deliver the project tomorrow.
MEANING	**What is the cause of these emotions?** That's a good question. John is very structured and I am not. Perhaps he feels that I am not taking the project as seriously as he is. I realize I haven't been giving him status updates and maybe he doesn't realize the work I've done and how close we are to finishing the project. I am at the point of collapse from exhaustion. Perhaps I'm overreacting but I can't help feel the way I do.
MOVE	**How will you sustain or move these emotions?** Instead of responding to the email, I am going to go see John in person. I plan on addressing his e-mail but before I meet him, I need to cool down so I am ready for his feedback. I will acknowledge he is upset with me and ask him why he feels the way he does. Instead of taking it personally and defending or attacking, I will listen carefully to see if there is anything I can do to rectify the situation. I will be positive but serious in conveying my confidence in the work I have done. I will admit I haven't been communicating as effectively as I should and will do so going forward. I will ask him for other suggestions on how we can work better together so this doesn't happen again.

DEALING WITH A
WORK BULLY

BACKGROUND I have been working with Devon, the head of IT, for several months now and he is a downright bully. I have watched him verbally abuse others but now he's focused on me. It can be very subtle such as making disparaging comments in meetings, ignoring me in the hallway or making little digs about my performance. I've reached my limit and if things don't change soon, who knows what I'll do.

GOAL Have a productive conversation with Devon so he will stop his bullying behavior.

EI BLUEPRINT

STRATEGIES USED Modify Mood; Reappraise; Select Situation; Emotional Connection.

OUTCOME Shortly after I decided to do something about the situation with Devon, he bullied me in a meeting. My immediate reaction was to shut down but then I reminded myself of my plan. I asked to meet with him later that day. I prepared by envisioning a positive meeting and practiced a lot of deep breathing to calm down. I thanked him for meeting me and mentioned I could sense he wasn't happy with my performance and wanted to know what we could do to work together more effectively. At first, Devon ignored me and kept saying not to take things so personally and he was only joking. However, I must give him credit, he could see how important working well together was to me and he listened. I told him how I wanted to have a collegial relationship and get to know him better. I suggested lunch the next day and we went. It was a little awkward at first, but we actually have quite a bit in common. I found out that he is an avid golfer and so am I and we agreed to go golfing soon. Over the next several weeks, as we got to know each other better, the bullying stopped and we haven't had an issue since. However, if he hadn't stopped this behavior, I would have discussed the situation with our Human Resources Director. No one should be bullied – ever

STEP	WHAT TO DO
MAP	**What are the emotions of you and others?** I feel *ashamed* that I haven't had the guts to stand up to Devon. I am *confused* why he is bullying me and *disappointed* a colleague of mine would treat me that way. I am also *angry* with Devon that he feels bullying is acceptable.
MATCH	**What emotions are most helpful?** I know how I feel right now is negatively impacting my productivity. I am avoiding Devon and our projects are falling behind. We should be working collaboratively and collegially and getting things done, not acting like school kids.
MEANING	**What is the cause of these emotions?** I was bullied as a kid and Devon's behavior is bringing back painful memories. I think Devon likes intimidating people and it makes him feel powerful and in control. Personally, I think he lacks self-confidence and his behavior is a result of something else going on in his life. But I could be wrong.
MOVE	**How will you sustain or move these emotions?** I realize that I have been judging Devon. I haven't really got to know him and I haven't practiced much empathy towards him either. Perhaps the reason he behaves the way he does is for other reasons besides him wanting to be a bully. The next time he bullies me, I am going to engage him on his behavior. I will not avoid him or meet him with anger because that won't resolve the issue. Instead, I will focus on our mutual goal. I will ask him questions around the topic. I will ask him what his expectations are of me and I will share mine of him. I will stay positive and appreciate Devon for his strengths and what he brings to the team. I will let him know I would like to have a collegial relationship with him and see if perhaps we can get to know each other better. Perhaps over lunch or a beer after work. I am confident that Devon will stop his behavior if we just get to know each other better.

DEALING WITH
UNCERTAINTY AND VOLATILITY

BACKGROUND Our company is in the middle of a major reorganization. This is our third one in less than 5 years. Our market keeps changing and we are struggling to keep up and stay ahead of our competition. As one of the senior vice presidents, my team is looking to me for reassurance, stability and support. I just hope I can deliver, or we'll all be looking for a job.

GOAL Help move the organization forward in a positive direction.

EI BLUEPRINT

STRATEGIES USED Modify Mood; Intervening Moment; Emotional Connection; Modulate Tone.

OUTCOME I had to step out of my comfort zone to share my concerns with my colleagues. I am not used to showing vulnerability and it was a little scary. But, once I did, others joined in and we all agreed we had a responsibility to step up and lead with vision and purpose. We agreed to have an all-hands meeting to re-engage and re-energize our employees. And, it wasn't fake. We knew we had to be genuine because they'd see right through us. The meeting allowed people to share their feelings and get excited about our future. It really was infectious and we left the meeting feeling hopeful and re-focused on a positive future. Since that meeting, we've seen significant improvement in morale and how we communicate with each other—even under stress. Another re-organization will happen again, but next time we'll know how to handle it.

STEP	WHAT TO DO
MAP	**What are the emotions of you and others?** Even though we've been through this before, this is *scary.* We are *anxious* and *worried* that we are going to lose our jobs. People are *agitated*, *frustrated* and *disappointed* that our company is losing ground and may become obsolete. And we're *tired* and *burned out* from working extra long hours.
MATCH	**What emotions will be most helpful?** Our moods are certainly overwhelming us and our behavior is only going to lead to our demise sooner rather than later. We have shut down on each other and communication is abysmal. The negativity is palpable and contagious and is infecting everyone in the company from top down. While we shouldn't be happy with the situation, we need to collaborate and support each other more effectively.
MEANING	**What is the cause of these emotions?** Our company has been one of the top companies in our sector for the past decade. We enjoyed major growth and profitability and watching it slip away is unbearable. It's easy to understand why we feel the way we do but how we are behaving is not going to get us to where we need to be.
MOVE	**How will you sustain or move these emotions?** As one of the executives, I need to address this situation with my peers. I need to facilitate a dialogue around what we are all experiencing so we address the impact our emotions are having on the company and our staff. We need to be role models for our employees. We need to recommit to our purpose and look to the future with positivity and hope. We need to inspire our employees and engage them in our vision of the future. We need to encourage open communication, inclusivity, transparency and positivity at all levels of our organization. However, it needs to start at the top. We are a great company with a great product and together we can figure out where and how to thrive in the future.

DELIVERING
UNWELCOMED NEWS

BACKGROUND We have a new product coming to market next month and everyone is on cloud 9. This is a big win for our company. As Chief Financial Officer, I am concerned we are spreading ourselves too thin. Adding to my concern is we have quality issues that may impact the launch. Our President is calling an executive meeting to discuss the new product release. Everyone is so positive, and no one is especially concerned about what I'm seeing. While not a pessimist, I see potential for this upcoming meeting to blow up.

GOAL Share concerns to engage the leadership team in a collaborative discussion.

EI BLUEPRINT

STRATEGIES USED Modify Mood; Express a Different Emotion; Emotional Connection.

OUTCOME At our next meeting I totally shocked everyone. Instead of handing out a report, I verbally shared our financial situation using emotion delivered with a bit more intensity than usual for me. They tried to focus me on the positive but I stayed on topic so they understood the seriousness of the situation and the negative impact it could have on our future. I got their attention. By showing up differently, it allowed us to enter a meaningful conversation on where we were and where we needed to be. We left the meeting fully understanding the issue and successfully launched the product—18 months later. During the delay we used the time to resolve quality and strengthen our bottom line.

STEP	WHAT TO DO
MAP	**What are the emotions of you and others?** I am *nervous* because I know I may be considered a troublemaker or even "Chicken Little". I am also *worried* if I don't bring up how I'm feeling, the company could experience bad publicity that hurts the company. My colleagues are *excited* and filled with *anticipation* that we have a new product hitting the market after 5 years in development.
MATCH	**What emotions are most helpful?** I know this meeting is going to be contentious and my worry will be viewed as a weakness. I need to address this situation in a factual manner and share my concerns in a way people won't feel defensive or shut me down. I am happy that my colleagues are so positive but it's distracting them from noticing what's really going on.
MEANING	**What is the cause of these emotions?** Our company has been doing great and life is good. Clients and employees seem happy and profit isn't great, but it's good. However, I've been reading industry reports warning us of lean times ahead. Our customers aren't buying new products and our bottom line is starting to shrink. I have brought this up several times in the boardroom and keep getting ignored. Now we are about to launch a new product that may have quality issues. We can't afford to make a mistake and this new development worries me.
MOVE	**How will you sustain or move these emotions?** As CFO, I am the numbers person and have been providing weekly reports showing our continued decline. I realize I have been unemotional about it and the reaction I get is also unemotional. Facts and figures do not convey a story. Therefore, I will switch up the way I usually present the material. I will share industry data, perhaps show a video related to our industry to show the shift we are all seeing. I don't want to panic them so I will remain calm, listen and allow time for information to sink in. Then I will engage them in a conversation on what we can do to address the data so we leave the meeting making the best decision for our company and customers.

LOSING
DRIVE AND PASSION FOR WORK

BACKGROUND I have worked for the same organization for over 32 years and am 4 years from retirement. I've held many jobs over my career and loved almost all of them. As head of financial operations of a multi-million dollar organization, I oversee a great team of 42 people. They are young, enthusiastic, smart and innovative. I know when I leave, they will carry on and be amazing leaders. Part of me wonders if it's time for me to move on now, rather than watching the clock tick down like others I have seen. Lately, I haven't been looking forward to work and while I love my team, I've lost my passion, motivation and enthusiasm. I thought I'd feel differently with time, but after almost a year, it's time to figure out what's really going on.

GOAL Re-engage and recommit to my job.

EI BLUEPRINT

STRATEGIES USED Modify Mood; Emotional Connection.

OUTCOME I ended up having a team meeting and was totally honest with them on how I've been feeling. I told them I wanted to end my career as their boss and needed to make some changes. I shared how much I enjoyed mentoring and I'd like to help them with their career development if they were interested. I was so pleased almost all of my team took me up on my offer. I also spoke with my boss and shared how I'd been feeling. Come to find out, our company was thinking about implementing a new financial system and needed someone to lead the project. She asked if I wanted to be the lead and I jumped. Now my days are chocked full of mentoring, leading the financial system project and working with my team. My drive is back and I can't wait to get to work every day—at least for the next 4 years!

STEP	WHAT TO DO
MAP	**What are the emotions of you and others?** I feel *tired*, *bored* and *disengaged* and I think my boss and team sense it as well. I am *worried* people will think I'm "retiring in place" and they want me to move on sooner rather than later.
MATCH	**What emotions are most helpful?** I hate feeling this way. This isn't me. I have always been passionate about the work I do. I want to get that feeling back again. Even worse, this low-energy state will not help me address my challenges. Instead I need to fully engage around this issue.
MEANING	**What is the cause of these emotions?** I've been with my company for over 30 years. My team are the experts and I sit back and watch them excel. I can do my job with my eyes closed. I'm bored and unchallenged and know my team won't miss me if I leave.
MOVE	**How will you sustain or move these emotions?** I had to reflect when I felt the happiest at work. What was I doing? Who was I with? I quickly realized I'm happiest when mentoring my team. Because I don't want to micromanage or interfere in their work, I've backed off from mentoring. I also haven't taken on a challenging project in years because I want my team to take the lead—it's their time to shine. I realize that I miss feeling useful. Instead of sitting back feeling sorry for myself it's time to take action.

PART THREE

QUESTIONS, ANSWERS, RESOURCES

WE HOPE THAT THESE BLUEPRINTS ARE HELPFUL TO YOU. If you read through them, you are likely to find a few that approximate your current challenges and with some figurative cutting and pasting, you can create a Blueprint that meets your specific needs. As you develop your own Blueprints contact us at blueprint@eiskills.com to share what you learned.

Leaders' Key Questions and Issues

We've worked with leaders around the world on the ability model of emotional intelligence, have heard hundreds of questions, objections and arguments. You may be highly skeptical of EI and its application to you or your organization. Let's tackle some of the questions and issues we've heard over the years.

Our Culture Will Not Support an "Emotional" Approach.
Smart, analytical people often have doubts about EI. So do we. If EI is presented as assertiveness, listening and "being

nice", we too would resist its introduction. However, in our approach emotions are data and a source of information. In our approach you harness the raw power of emotions to accomplish difficult goals. And, we emphasize that all emotions—sadness, anxiety, anger, happiness and others—can be adaptive, helpful and smart.

I Can't Ask People "how are you feeling?"

Then ask another question. We recognize your culture may not allow such a direct question. Instead, come up with your own way of asking, perhaps focusing on tone, or modeling this yourself. For example, when asked "how are you?" you might respond "good, but a bit worried about the sales forecast meeting and not sure how to prep for it". We've both worked with bureaucratic, formal organizations and have been impressed with ways to ask the "how are you?" question that do not violate the behavioral norms of those organizations.

We Believe in 'Strong Leadership', Not Emotional Leadership.

We hear this one a lot, especially outside the U.S. Strong leaders instill a sense of urgency and pride in their organization. Urgency is generated from anxiety (an emotion) and pride (a strong emotion). Strong leaders know this and EI can underpin strong leadership. EI leaders are not sobbing at meetings and talking about feelings all the time. They leverage and harness the power of emotions to achieve goals. The key is you need to tap into the power of emotions with great sophistication.

We've Already Done This.

You may have run a session on EI but our guess is you have not trained on the ability model where emotions are data and helpful in decision making. Consider a hard-skills approach to EI with the use of the Blueprint and the four abilities of emotional intelligence.

These Blueprints Seem Pretty Easy.

They are—once you lay out the challenge and focus on the underlying emotional causes. The challenge for you is to address leadership problems in the moment, or even better, to use a structured approach to emotion-based problem solving to avoid creating a problem in the first place. Each Blueprint is easy on its own, but we find that it takes a lot of skill as well as a great deal of effort to consistently and effectively leverage EI in every critical situation.

How Do I Hire for EI?

It's not easy. EI is not always visible. You could use our ability test, the MSCEIT; but if you do, be very careful. Start with a job analysis. If that provides you with support for the notion EI is a critical job skill, then go ahead. If you use the MSCEIT let the results help you target interview questions. Never hire based on an assessment alone.

Are You Saying Anger is Helpful?

Anger can fuel change but acting angrily is almost always a bad idea. Anger is a corrosive and dangerous emotion. You need highly-advanced emotion management skills to be an effective manager of anger. Nothing in this book gives you permission to be a jerk! You can only harness the power of anger for social justice if you are a master of emotions, and frankly, few of us are. Consider the examples of people like Rosa Parks, Dr. King or Mahatma Gandhi to illustrate how hard and rare it is to leverage the power of anger in the service of a larger cause.

Can EI Be Used Negatively?

Can you use these skills to manipulate people? Unfortunately, perhaps you can and that concerns us. Properly used, these skills result in positive outcomes for everyone, but in the wrong hands, it is possible to wreak havoc on the lives of people. But it is unlikely, and there are several reasons for this. Some data exist to suggest that high EI people score lower on Machiavellianism, for example. High EI people have better long-term quality relationships which means they are not using their abilities for evil purposes. Empathy plays a role here as well -- if I feel your pain I will not intentionally harm you. At the same time, there are a few studies that people high on emotion management and Machiavellianism can and do use their ability to manipulate people.

I Find It Hard to Generate Positive Emotions, Is That a Problem?

Few of us can process all emotions equally well. Some people tend to live in the "middle" of the Mood Map and don't experience strong emotions or swings. But if you find it difficult to generate positive emotions and find yourself feeling sad much of the time, you should certainly consult a professional.

The American Psychological Association has a search function on its website at http://www.apa.org/helpcenter/.

Should I Always Follow This Approach?

Absolutely not. We've included a few cases about a volatile boss and a bully. Let us be clear that in no case should you tolerate such behavior. If the blueprint approach does not work, you must take action which means referring the unacceptable situation to a senior executive or a trusted HR professional.

ADDITIONAL RESOURCES

Measuring Emotional Intelligence—There are three ways to measure an ability: you can ask people to provide their own estimate, you can ask others to estimate a person's ability or you can give the person an ability test. Once you select the overall method, you then need to develop test items that measure EI according to how you define EI. For us, the best way to measure EI is with an ability test where items measure Perceive (Map), Facilitate/Use (Match), Understand (Meaning), and Manage (Move). The Mayer, Salovey, Caruso Emotional Intelligence Test (MSCEIT) does just this. It's a bit unusual but it often provides interesting insights into your EI skills.

Books—We have a book on EI, *The Emotionally Intelligent Manager*, but there are many other books as well, although they view EI differently than we do. The book that catapulted the concept into the public sphere is Goleman's *Emotional Intelligence.* While Goleman stretched the concept of EI, his book is very well written. A book that focuses on EI in the workplace is *Emotional Intelligence 2.0,* although its focus differs from ours. Our friends at 6 Seconds (6seconds.org) have many valuable resources.

Research Articles—If you are interested in exploring some of the research behind the concepts in our book, consider starting with some of these articles. As you explore the field, do take care to read the full article in order to understand how the researcher is defining and measuring emotional intelligence.

Cote, S., DeCelles, K. A., McCarthy, J. M., Van Kleef, G. A., & Hideg, I. (2011). The Jekyll and Hyde of emotional intelligence: Emotion-regulation knowledge facilitates both prosocial and interpersonally deviant behavior. Psychological Science, 22, 1073-1080.

Joseph, D. L., & Newman, D. A. (2010). Emotional intelligence: An integrative meta-analysis and cascading model. Journal of Applied Psychology, 95(1), 54-78. doi:10.1037/a0017286.

MacCann, C., Joseph, D., Newman, D., Roberts, R. (2014). Emotional Intelligence Is a Second-Stratum Factor of Intelligence: Evidence From Hierarchical and Bifactor Models. Emotion, 14(2), 358-374.

Mayer, J. D., Caruso, D. R., & Salovey, P. (2016). The ability model of emotional intelligence: Principles and updates. Emotion Review, 8, 1-11.

Mayer, J. D., & Salovey, P. (1997). What is emotional intelligence? In D. J. Sluyter (Ed.), Emotional development and emotional intelligence: Educational implications. (pp. 3-34). New York, NY US: Basic Books.

Sheldon, O.J., Dunning, D., & Ames, D.R. (2014). Emotionally unskilled, unaware, and uninterested in learning more: Reactions to feedback about deficits in emotional intelligence. Journal of Applied Psychology, 99, 125-137.

Websites—Websites on EI abound and here is a plug for our sites: ltrleadership.com and eiskillsgroup.com. Also see Jack Mayer's site at http://mypages.unh.edu/jdmayer.

Organizations—Organizations or groups focused on emotional intelligence include the following:

- The Consortium for Research on Emotional Intelligence in Organizations (http://www.eiconsortium.org/)
- International Society for Emotional Intelligence (http://www.emotionalintelligencesociety.org/)

ABOUT THE AUTHORS

David R. Caruso, Ph.D.

David is the co-founder of Emotional Intelligence (EI) Skills Group. In addition, he is the Senior Advisor to the Dean of Yale College and a research affiliate at the Yale Center for Emotional Intelligence. David is the co-author of the Mayer, Salovey, Caruso Emotional Intelligence Tests (MSCEIT, MSCEIT Youth Research Version and MSCEIT 2).

He and colleague Peter Salovey wrote The Emotionally Intelligent Manager, and he is a co-author of The Anchors of Emotional Intelligence school program (aka "Ruler") (Brackett, Caruso & Stern). David has published numerous articles – peer reviewed journal articles, reviews and chapters - on the topics of emotional intelligence and leadership. He has trained thousands of professionals around the world.

David received his Ph.D. in psychology from Case Western Reserve University and was awarded a two-year postdoctoral fellowship in psychology at Yale University.

David has also held positions in market research, strategic planning, and product management, led numerous product development teams, conducted sales training seminars, developed and implemented marketing plans and introduced new products in the United States and Europe.

Contact: david@eiskills.com

Lisa T. Rees, ACC, MPA

Lisa is the principal of LTR Leadership, specializing in helping leaders and their teams develop skills to build trust. She provides consulting, facilitates workshops, and coaches using emotional intelligence (EI) and appreciative inquiry (AI) as the foundation for her practice. Lisa was a manager, leader, coach, and instructor with the U.S. Citizenship and Immigration Services (USCIS). While there, Lisa led teams in implementing financial systems and cost efficiencies throughout her agency before switching career fields to become a certified leadership coach in 2015. Lisa has an A.S. in Accounting and a B.S. in Management from Champlain College and her Master in Public Administration from Norwich University. Lisa is certified in the Mayer Salovey Caruso Emotional Intelligence Test (MSCEIT) as well as certified in Appreciative Inquiry (AI) and numerous leadership assessment tools. Lisa is a strategic partner with the David L. Cooperrider Center of Appreciative Inquiry and is a guest instructor at the Naval Postgraduate School. Lisa and David are frequent collaborators and have written several books and journal articles, developed an EI course for Udemy, and certify people in the MSCEIT.

Contact: lisa@ltrleadership.com.

ACKNOWLEDGEMENTS

EMOTIONS FORM THE BASIS OF RELATIONSHIPS, AND, AS it turns out, relationships created emotional intelligence. John (Jack) Mayer and David were fellow grad students in their Ph.D. program at Case Western Reserve University. David met Peter Salovey when Peter was a grad student at Yale where David was a postdoctoral fellow in psychology. Jack and Peter met separately at emotions conferences and found they had many things in common. From their informal discussions came their theory of emotional intelligence.

Lisa and David met in 2011 when she took one of his MSCEIT certification workshops and now they co-teach MSCEIT workshops and are friends. Although we acknowledge Jack and Peter's contributions, this book is our own and we take sole responsibility for claims, errors and omissions.

We are grateful to Tere Gade for her editing help (and we take responsibility for any issues with our book!). Finally, thanks to Adam Robinson of Good Book Developers for turning our vision from a document into a book.